The Ignatian
Workout for Lent

Other Books by Tim Muldoon

The Ignatian Workout

Longing to Love

The Ignatian Workout for Lent

40 Days of Prayer, Reflection, and Action

TIM MULDOON

LOYOLA PRESS.
A JESUIT MINISTRY
Chicago

LOYOLA PRESS.
A JESUIT MINISTRY

3441 N. Ashland Avenue
Chicago, Illinois 60657
(800) 621-1008
www.loyolapress.com

Scripture quotations are taken from the *New Revised Standard Version Bible*, copyright © 1989, Division of Christian Education of the National Council of the Churches of Christ in the United States of America. Used by permission. All rights reserved.

Cover art credit: Johner Images/Hakan Hjort/Media Bakery.

ISBN-13: 978-0-8294-4039-3
Library of Congress Control Number: 2013950593

Printed in the United States of America.
20 21 22 23 24 25 26 27 28 29 Bang 13 12 11 10 9 8 7 6 5 4

Forgetting what lies behind and straining forward to what lies ahead, I press on toward the goal for the prize of the heavenly call of God in Christ Jesus.

—Philippians 3:13–14

Contents

Introduction: Becoming a Spiritual Athlete

In several places, St. Paul uses the metaphor of athletics to draw an analogy to the spiritual life of the followers of Christ. In his letter to the church in the Macedonian city of Philippi, for example, he writes the following:

I want to know Christ and the power of his resurrection and the sharing of his sufferings by becoming like him in his death, if somehow I may attain the resurrection from the dead. Not that I have already obtained this or have already reached the goal; but I press on to make it my own, because Christ Jesus has made me his own. Beloved, I do not consider that I have made it my own; but this one thing I do: forgetting what lies behind and straining forward to what lies ahead, I press on toward the goal for the prize of the heavenly call of God in Christ Jesus.

—Philippians 3:10–14

I have been struck by this image of "pressing on toward the goal" for many years—ever since I found it emblazoned on a poster that someone gave me at the height of my athletic training in college. Immediately I drew a connection that, decades later, has stayed with me: life in Christ demands the same kind of vigilance, preparation, and training that a person undertakes as an athlete.

Elsewhere, in a letter he wrote to some Christians in the Greek city of Corinth, Paul suggests an image for how to think about the way to live in the hope of heaven:

Do you not know that in a race the runners all compete, but only one receives the prize? Run in such a way that you may win it. Athletes exercise self-control in all things; they do it to receive a perishable wreath, but we an imperishable one. So I do not run aimlessly, nor do I box as though beating the air; but I punish my body and enslave it, so that after proclaiming to others I myself should not be disqualified.
—1 Corinthians 9:24–27

Paul's suggestion that discipleship is like training for a running race or a boxing match calls to mind several points. First, he suggests that it is necessary to maintain focus on a goal rather than be distracted by whatever passing pleasures, rest, or pointless wastes of time get in the way. Second, he reminds the Christ followers that their goal is infinitely greater than the prizes that athletes of his time received—a laurel crown (the "perishable wreath"). Third, he suggests that Christians are in a kind of competition with others. Today, we might consider that in academia, in the blogosphere, and in popular media such as television, film, and journalism, there is a constant competition for market share, and that it is a challenge for anyone who would seek to get a message across to outwork and outdistance others who similarly devote themselves to proclaiming their truths.

By the second century, a tradition of "spiritual athletes" began to develop in the church, especially among Syriac Christians in the lands of modern-day Turkey and Iraq. Figures such as Ephrem, Isaac of Nineveh, and Simeon the Stylite lived the most sparse lifestyles in order to show the kind of focus St. Paul called for. Their "spiritual exercises," not unlike those of pre-Christian philosophers such as the Stoics and Epicureans (not to mention Buddhists, followers of the Tao, and many others), were ordered toward a higher good, analogous to the goods that Olympic athletes pursued. What the spiritual athletes sought to tame were the desires of the flesh—gluttony, drunkenness, lust, and the like—that hindered them from their pursuit of glory.

It is not surprising that the key figure in the development of (Western) Catholic theology in the early church, St. Augustine, similarly relied on the wisdom of St. Paul. This rhetorician and philosopher experienced a process of conversion that emerged through a slow recognition of his own dissipation and the recognition that his spiritual life lacked a center and a goal. His long, slow growth toward Christ involved coming to see how stuck he was in meaningless desires, especially lust. In today's language, he realized he had an addiction, and he sought freedom from it. His final experience of falling in love with Christ brought that freedom, one that allowed him to let go of his addiction and embrace a call to love, to leadership, and to the service of the faithful through his voluminous writings.

Centuries later, another young man found himself in a position similar to that of Augustine, realizing that he, too, had been captive to pointless desires, in restless conformity to the zeitgeist. Only a painful process of convalescence after a war injury gave the young Íñigo Loiolakoa (later Ignatius of Loyola) a wider-lens view: that beneath the desires the world told him he should have were quieter, yet more lasting and beautiful, desires planted as seeds by a God who loved him. Eventually Íñigo would pen the *Spiritual Exercises*, which offered others an expcrience of careful attention to God that Ignatius had found so transformative. Describing the exercises, he suggests that they are to help us know the difference between true and false desire: "to overcome oneself, and to order one's life, without reaching a decision through some disordered affection [*afección desordenada*]." Put most simply, Íñigo wanted to help people see through false desires to the true ones that most purely revealed God's love for us. For him, spiritual exercises were not about earning God's love; they were about removing the detours that distract us from knowing it intimately.

Ignatius lived a life that enabled him to understand this basic pattern. Like all of us, he spent his youth glancing around nervously at everyone else. He imitated what he saw and became good at these things, these "vanities," as he later called them, What changed everything was a catastrophe: a horrible injury that left him broken and bereft, forced to turn inside to ask what sort of life he would live. The answer emerged slowly and painfully: he learned to see the massive difference between the flash points of temporary highs and the slow but lasting peace of authentic desires rooted in God. He spent the rest of his life marinating in those authentic desires, sharing his exercises with those who would similarly live a meaning-saturated life.

The exercises in this book are indebted to this charismatic Spaniard who taught us how to discern true desire from false. Rooted in the ancient practices of imitation of Christ and the saints, the exercises invite us to drink deeply from the wells of our imagination, that portal through which God's voice echoes with images and poetry that elude rational calculation. Ignatius discovered God more as a beloved than as a theorem, and so invited others to encounter the same God not through cleverness or study but through simple attentiveness to the reality of their own lives. To slow down, as it were, long enough to take a long, loving look at the real.[1]

This book takes as its point of departure a view of the spiritual life that sees various forms of prayer as exercises that help us see the world the way God does. This view is both ancient and new: it reaches back to the earliest days of the church, when Christians would gather to remember the words of Jesus using prayers he had taught them. Yet it is also contemporary, reflecting the practice of so many millions of Christians who set aside time, especially during the penitential period of Lent, to refocus their energies on kindling into flame the embers of their relationship with God.

The first thing to remember, then, is that a spiritual workout is very unlike physical workouts in one

---

1. The phrase "long, loving look at the real" comes from the Carmelite William McNamara, describing contemplation, but also from the essay of the same title by Walter Burghardt, SJ, reprinted in George W. Traub, SJ, ed., *An Ignatian Spirituality Reader* (Chicago: Loyola Press, 2008), 89–98.

important respect: *we don't make ourselves spiritual people by working hard.* That idea looks more like building our egos so that we can more easily frown on those who don't work quite as hard as we do. That was the error of the Pharisee who looked down on the tax collector:

[Jesus] also told this parable to some who trusted in themselves that they were righteous and regarded others with contempt: "Two men went up to the temple to pray, one a Pharisee and the other a tax collector. The Pharisee, standing by himself, was praying thus, 'God, I thank you that I am not like other people: thieves, rogues, adulterers, or even like this tax collector. I fast twice a week; I give a tenth of all my income.' But the tax collector, standing far off, would not even look up to heaven, but was beating his breast and saying, 'God, be merciful to me, a sinner!' I tell you, this man went down to his home justified rather than the other; for all who exalt themselves will be humbled, but all who humble themselves will be exalted."

—Luke 18:9–14

Jesus wants to disabuse his listeners of the fiction that multiplying good actions is the most direct way to heaven. Spiritual workouts are not about becoming better than others in some divine competition in which only the strong survive to make it into heaven. Rather, spiritual workouts are about removing obstacles to God's grace so that God can draw us closer to himself and make us capable of serving him. Those obstacles are always rooted in false desire, by which I mean cravings for things that, in the long run, do us or humanity no good.

A second thing to remember is that authentic spirituality always has an "ecclesial" dimension—that is, it is always ordered not toward my isolated personal good, but rather toward the good of the whole people of God. Imagine for a moment a member of a large family who lives together in a big house. She might have a strong desire that she discerns to be a vocational call by God to be a filmmaker. That desire may be rooted in a desire to serve others; it may draw on her talents; it may give her great joy. But if that desire moves her to wield control over the one TV in the living room all the time, she is acting in a disordered way. She must, as a member of the family, look for the "narrow way" that allows her to cultivate her vocation and also recognize the legitimate concerns of the rest of her family. That narrow way will involve always asking the question, How is God using my desires to serve my family and the rest of the world?

We must work hard at spiritual workouts because we live in cultures that too often exalt the individual at the expense of the common good; that elicit false desires so that we will go out and buy the latest item to satisfy them; that carve up the world into balkanized minorities through sins of racism or sexism or various nationalisms; that exalt wealth and power and sexual irresponsibility. As social creatures, we constantly glance around nervously at others for a sense of place in the world, imitating social patterns whether or not they ultimately serve the good. We crave what others crave and find ourselves exercising "common sense"—a euphemism for unthinking imitation—to justify going after what we want. We often experience our desires as things we cannot live without. We are trapped by desire.

The old monkey-trap story can be helpful. In order to catch a monkey, goes the story, all you need to do is put a banana in a jar just wide enough for a monkey's hand to reach through. The monkey, seizing the banana, will try to draw his hand out in order to claim the prize, but his fist wrapped around the banana will prevent him from ever extricating himself from the jar. The craving for the banana strangles the monkey's freedom.

All of us have a tendency to be like the monkey (and like Augustine and Ignatius): to tie our happiness to fleeting desires rather than to the one source of joy that will make us free. We become distracted from the task of soldiering on through difficulties and sufferings and latch onto what will give us temporary happiness. Spiritual workouts, then, are about training ourselves to let go of false desires so that we can respond to God more freely. Only then can we love and serve God and God's purposes in the world. And what we find is that in the place of temporary happiness grows something quieter, more profound, and lasting: joy. I believe that this is what Jesus was speaking about when he told people that the kingdom of God is near.

What follows are forty exercises—four groups of ten—designed to help pilgrims remove the obstacles to grace and to cultivate greater attentiveness to the really real. This attentiveness will neither remove suffering from life nor offer an abstract notion of heaven that takes away the responsibility and freedom to live the lives God has given us. Rather, these exercises are about keeping our eyes on God, in whose "light we see light" (Psalm 36:9)—that is to say, they are about seeing our lives, our struggles and sufferings, our joys and our hopes, in the light of the great work that God has called us to unfold around us. This way of taking a "long, loving look at the real" can help us face both joy and suffering with the right sense of purpose, not unlike a marathoner who faces both easy stretches and difficulties en route to his goal. During periods of facility and difficulty, consolation and desolation, the runner can exclaim with Paul, "I press on toward the goal for the prize of the heavenly call of God in Christ Jesus" (Philippians 3:14).

The forty exercises are designed to reflect two complementary approaches. The first is that of the church's celebration of the Lenten season, the forty days of prayer, fasting, and repentance rooted in ancient Israelite practices. Forty is a biblical number: Israelites wandering in the desert for forty years; Jesus fasting for forty days in the wilderness before his public ministry. Forty days represents a period of conversion, of serious preparation for a new way of living.

The second approach is that of St. Ignatius in his book *Spiritual Exercises*. He divides the period of intense prayer into four "weeks," which can last an actual week or longer, in order to distinguish four interrelated movements of growth in relationship with God. The four groups of ten exercises reflect this basic Ignatian approach.[2]

The first group of ten exercises focuses on the theme of seeing myself as God sees me. The texts from this group of exercises are about getting a "God's-eye view" and getting out of the patterns that prevent me from seeing myself as a beloved child of God. The emphasis in this first group is on seeing myself and the world as it really is rather than through the distorted lenses of false desires.

The second group focuses on choosing to follow the beautiful paradox that is Christ. This group

---

2. For an introduction to Ignatian spiritual exercises, see my earlier book *The Ignatian Workout* (Chicago: Loyola Press, 2004), upon which this book is based.

invites us to see him as the paradigm of faith, the one who shows us the way to trust God even in the face of suffering, for the sake of a love that saves us.

The third group follows the logic of that call of Christ: in following him and choosing to open our hearts in love, we will without fail experience suffering. Love opens our hearts to desire the good of the other, even as it opens us to receive the pains that the other receives. We experience Christ's death as the outcome of his love for us.

Finally, the fourth group calls to mind the fact that love is the aim of all our spiritual exercises, that in the end God calls us not to suffering as an end in itself but as the path through which we travel to deeper joy. We rejoice with Christ in his resurrection and remember that in conquering death he has released us from the fear that our love might be in vain.

Each of the forty exercises involves a short text, a meditation, a recommendation for prayer, and an action—that we might be both hearers and doers of the word (see James 1:22). I suggest you do no more than one exercise per day. You may want to return to the same exercise more than once in a day—perhaps upon waking, and again before sleeping. If it is fruitful, return to it again another day. Don't worry if you miss a day; just return the next day and carry on. The objective is not to race through them but rather to approach them as aids to your ongoing conversation with God. As a final note, if you begin with exercise 1 on a Monday, you'll do exercise 6 (which recommends sacramental confession) on a Saturday, which is the day when many parishes offer the sacrament.

First

God Has Created Me for Some Good

Let me learn to listen to God by eliminating the noise in my life that drowns out his voice.

Exercise 1

I Know the Plans I Have for You

†

I know the plans I have for you, says the LORD, plans for your welfare and not for harm, to give you a future with hope. Then when you call upon me and come and pray to me, I will hear you. When you search for me, you will find me; if you seek me with all your heart, I will let you find me, says the LORD, and I will restore your fortunes and gather you from all the nations and all the places where I have driven you, says the LORD, and I will bring you back to the place from which I sent you into exile.

—Jeremiah 29:11–14

The prophet Jeremiah was writing to the people of Israel during the worst time anyone could remember: they had been sent into exile after having been conquered by Babylon. "God has abandoned us!" some would have shouted. Others would have questioned even that kind of loyalty, saying, "Our God is weak. He could not protect us."

There is a good bit of evidence that ancient Israelites had all sorts of different understandings of who God was and what he could do. Like us, they doubted, they got angry at God, and they questioned whether he was worth believing in. Jeremiah's words come in the midst of a remarkable text that counsels them not to lose hope, even though they have been punished for their waywardness. Jeremiah says, effectively, to settle down for a couple of generations, till God calls Israel back.

Much of the language associated with Jeremiah is that of lament, a kind of complaint that God's ways are unfair.

> O that my head were a spring of water,
>   and my eyes a fountain of tears,
> so that I might weep day and night

for the slain of my poor people!

—Jeremiah 9:1

Jeremiah faces the grim reality of the world filled with suffering and pain, and he cries out to God in his distress. What is important to remember, though, is that his language—and indeed the language of many other Old Testament texts—is still spoken *to God*. This is not the language of unbelief or of cynicism; rather, it is the honest cry of the heart toward that which it cannot comprehend. This is not whitewashed piety of the "everything will turn out fine" variety, the empty words we sometimes throw around in the face of grief. This is the heart-wrenching, honest language of a man who sometimes abhors what he sees around him. He is honest enough to admit that sometimes he does not like God.

Recently one of my children was having a hard time adjusting to the presence of a new family member in our home. She was acting out in strange ways, and my wife and I came to realize that it was because she was lamenting the loss of Mom and Dad time. We decided it was important to give her some time, to help her name the source of her sadness and frustration—to allow her to speak her anger, as did Jeremiah. Our response was to offer her hope: we told her it was good to express her lament, that it was good not to hide it (this is good psychology, too). But we tried to help her imagine that, over time, a new kind of happiness would emerge.

The language that God speaks to his people is like our words to our daughter. "I know the plans I have for you . . . plans for your welfare and not for harm, to give you a future with hope." Hope does not ignore the reality of the world; it simply offers a change in perspective. Our faith is not blind insistence that everything is always fine; it is reliance on a God who offers us hope. Our faith is that God knows us better than we know ourselves, because we can see only what happens moment to moment.

Prayer

Spend time looking back over the past several weeks, and pay attention to where you are in your relationship with God. Do you trust him? What are your feelings toward God now? Are you grateful, angry, hopeful, grieving, excited, lethargic? What events or relationships have contributed to these feelings? Acknowledge them and speak them honestly. Write what you are feeling as words of prayer, whether of lament or thanksgiving or praise. Sit with God and speak honestly about what you lament, and allow God to speak back to you the words of hope from Jeremiah.

Action

Offer a word of hope to someone in your life today: perhaps a friend or a spouse or a child. Write a personal letter or a message; send a picture or a song; share a moving image on your favorite social-media site. Be for someone else the kind of person you want God to be for you today.

Exercise 2

You Have Searched Me and You Know Me

✝

O LORD, you have searched me and known me.
You know when I sit down and when I rise up;
*   you discern my thoughts from far away.*
You search out my path and my lying down,
*   and are acquainted with all my ways.*
Even before a word is on my tongue,
*   O LORD, you know it completely.*
You hem me in, behind and before,
*   and lay your hand upon me.*
Such knowledge is too wonderful for me;
*   it is so high that I cannot attain it.*

—Psalm 139:1–6

The psalmist expresses in these words a calm yet awed trust that God knows and loves everything about him. He gives words to the wonder, the mystery of his very self. Later in this psalm we see a similar sentiment: "I am fearfully and wonderfully made" (14).

I imagine this psalm emerging as the fruit of a period of quiet meditation, perhaps as the psalmist lay on the grass and gazed at the clouds on a beautiful summer day. Have you ever had a feeling of awe at the world? Do you remember feeling that way as a child—a sense that there is something overwhelming about the very existence of everything, and that your very being is part of what is so awe inspiring?

It is easy in the midst of a busy life to lose that sense of awe. The image that comes to mind is that of a mountain climber who begins the day by surveying the height of the mountain, taking in its beauty and grandeur, savoring the opportunity to climb. As she begins the climb, though, the work of navigating the terrain makes her lose sight of the summit. If the climb is especially difficult, she may forget about the beauty altogether and focus only on the immediate task of staying safe. It may take a pause in a place where she can see the summit to remind her of what her journey is really about.

Today, take a pause from your climb and survey the landscape. Imagine God looking at your life the way a novelist looks at a character in his novel: seeing the whole story in his imagination, enjoying the characters he has lovingly created. What delights God when he looks at you? What does God hope for you? What work is God trying to accomplish in you?

Or take another image, of a sculptor lovingly chiseling away at a block of marble that is you. What beauty does God see in the unfinished block of marble? What is God chipping away with each strike of the hammer? Does it cause pain? What will the finished sculpture look like? Can you express to God your honest feelings about the process? Can you trust the sculptor to give life to the vision?

Prayer

Pray the words of Psalm 139 slowly, speaking to God. Imagine God as a novelist and you a character in the novel, or God as a sculptor working to create you. What feelings emerge as you imagine these things? Tell God what you hope for and what you fear as God labors to bring you to greater life.

Action

Choose something to create: a recipe, a sculpture, a model airplane, a poem, a painting, a birdhouse, a film, or something else that draws on your talents. Give your creation to someone you love and tell him or her why you did it. Do everything you can to make the gift beautiful and remarkable so that the person understands that you gave your best effort on his or her behalf.

Exercise 3

My Soul Longs for You

†

As a deer longs for flowing streams,
*   so my soul longs for you, O God.*
My soul thirsts for God,
*   for the living God.*
When shall I come and behold
*   the face of God?*

—Psalm 42:1–2

Jews all over the world recite this psalm during the festival of Sukkot (the feast of tents, *sukkah*). This festival is a recollection of Israel's forty years of wandering in the desert, living in *sukkah* after their exodus from slavery in Egypt. For seven or eight days, Jews will eat and sometimes sleep in the *sukkah* and call to mind the longing for home that their ancestors would have felt as refugees. The expression of longing in this psalm may be understood as that longing for home.

The plight of refugees today may shed some light on what the psalmist is expressing in these lines. Listen to what one man, Sabir al-Zebeir, said of his experience fleeing genocide in Sudan:

> In 2005 the Government of Sudan and the Janjaweed militia attacked my village and burned everything down. . . . I tried to go to Chad, but government forces blocked the way; so I came to Ethiopia. When I came here I first went to a refugee camp, and was there almost two years. There was no security there and no services, so I came to Addis. . . . From morning to night we don't have anything, so we come here [the JRS community center]. . . . We want to learn and we

want to be in peace. But right now we have no education and we have no job.[3]

What Sabir expresses is a deep-heart longing shared
with all those who are in the difficult situation of
exile. That is close to what the psalmist points to in
the lines above: the feeling that the place in which we
find ourselves is not our true home.

Whether you are in a peaceful home or completely
homeless; around people who love you or alone; in
a good job or school or in a situation of dependence
on others—where is your deep-heart longing? How
do you find yourself reacting to things going on in
the world around you? When have you found yourself moved, or your heart broken? Where have you
reached out in sympathy for one who is suffering
what you have suffered, or in empathy toward someone whose pain is unknown to you personally but to
whom you wish to show mercy? That is where you
will meet God. Bring it into prayer.

---

3. Sabir al-Zebeir, quoted in Jesuit Refugee Service, "A Tale of Three
Cities: JRS Responds to the Needs of Refugees in Urban Environ-
ments," *Refugee Voice* (July 11, 2011).

Prayer

Name your experiences of heart longing, and give yourself time to write about why God has made your heart capable of such feeling. Ask God to lead you to tho home you long for, and the grace to bring others there with you.

Action

Talk to loved ones about the source of your heart longing, and learn what talents they see in you that might bring mercy to others.

Exercise 4

God Is Love

✝

Beloved, let us love one another, because love is from God; everyone who loves is born of God and knows God. Whoever does not love does not know God, for God is love. God's love was revealed among us in this way: God sent his only Son into the world so that we might live through him. In this is love, not that we loved God but that he loved us and sent his Son to be the atoning sacrifice for our sins. Beloved, since God loved us so much, we also ought to love one another. No one has ever seen God; if we love one another, God lives in us, and his love is perfected in us.

—1 John 4:7–12

Our deepest longings always point us toward love, and our longings for authentic love always point us toward God. What the author of John's first letter expresses is a truth we often dance around in our hopes for goodness in the world: our hopes for an end to violence; a perfect justice between men and women and children across the world; enough food and water to satisfy all hungers and thirsts. We sense deeply that *there is goodness*, that God must be present if the world is to have any meaning whatsoever, and that mindless cruelty is not the direction of human affairs. In John's language, love is from God.

The great paradox of the Christian mystery is that God has not put an end to violence and injustice; God instead has elected to suffer with us. How often we wish that God had chosen another way, the way of power over human choosing! For through our choices we lacerate our relationships with one another: we manipulate one another for money, for sexual pleasure, and for power. Through our choices we build our own nests while millions live on a dollar a day. God did not come to veto our choices but rather to suffer the consequences of our choices. "I was hungry and you gave me no food," Jesus says, for "just as you did not do it to one of the least of these [people], you did not do it to me" (Matthew 25:42, 45).

But this paradox implies that God's love *is* God's justice: before one who loves us *without any condition whatsoever*, we stand naked with empty hands. There is nothing we can offer but ourselves. We can continue to receive God's gifts and squander them, much like the prodigal son who takes his father's inheritance and runs off for a good time (Luke 15:11–32). Yet this God who has made our hearts for love will never be satisfied until we can truly receive that love and return it with our whole hearts. The Lord says, "I have swept away your transgressions like a cloud, and your sins like mist; return to me, for I have redeemed you" (Isaiah 44:22).

Prayer

Meditate on the final line above: "if we love one another, God lives in us, and his love is perfected in us." Where have you experienced love, either in giving or in receiving? Speak to God of what stirs in you as you consider that experience.

Action

Practice unselfish love by committing yourself to a thoughtful act for a friend or family member. Build that practice into a daily or weekly habit, and bring that act into prayer every day.

Exercise 5

I Do What I Hate

✝

I do not understand my own actions. For I do not do what I want, but I do the very thing I hate.

—Romans 7:15

Acknowledging sin is hard, but it is absolutely necessary.

Let me draw a comparison. Imagine for a moment that we completely shut our eyes to the possibility that our habits of consumption were causing harm to the environment. We continued to use gas-guzzling cars, we kept buying energy-sucking appliances and producing massive amounts of trash. If no one ever said to us, "Stop! We're producing acid rain! We're creating huge landfills! We're deforesting and losing topsoil! And poor people are losing farmland!" we would go on doing whatever appeared most convenient to us.

Or take another example: we kept on buying coffee and clothing without any concern for how our policies of trade were affecting poor farmers in South America or garment workers in Bangladesh. Rapacious middlemen would keep paying the farmers meager wages, while they charged $6 a cup for a massive latte or $30 for a sweatshirt, while migrant workers were mistreated and illegal buildings crashed to the ground, killing scores.

In both cases, it takes someone saying, "This is wrong" before anyone decides to change. The effects of the bad actions—sins—continue.

What Paul acknowledges in his letter to the Romans, in which we find this small but poignant observation, is that everyone tends to fall into habits that in many cases bring about results that we hate. More important, we may not recognize that those things are bad until someone draws the connection. But once they do, we face a dilemma. Do we accept the consequences of our actions and change our ways (the biblical word is "repent")? Or do we tend to criticize the messenger and accuse him or her of being politically backward?

Paul reminds us that we are not always totally in charge of our choices and that it takes prayer and reliance on God's grace to bring about the good. We can't just will it into being, because our desires often strangle us.

But because we acknowledge that sometimes we do what we hate and develop habits that are destructive even when we may not be aware of it, we need to inform our consciences and pray for grace.

Prayer

Spend time meditating on your tendency toward a particular sin—something for which the church calls us to repentance—and ask God to show you a new direction.

Action

Develop your conscience by reading the church's reflection on that sin (examples include the *Catechism of the Catholic Church* as well as other documents, such as writings of the saints). Pay attention to those areas in which you find yourself reacting against the church's wisdom; spend time learning the history of that issue and why the church teaches what it does.

Exercise 6

Depart from Me, a Sinner

†

When [Jesus] had finished speaking, he said to Simon, "Put out into the deep water and let down your nets for a catch." Simon answered, "Master, we have worked all night long but have caught nothing. Yet if you say so, I will let down the nets." When they had done this, they caught so many fish that their nets were beginning to break. So they signaled their partners in the other boat to come and help them. And they came and filled both boats, so that they began to sink. But when Simon Peter saw it, he fell down at Jesus' knees, saying, "Go away from me, Lord, for I am a sinful man!"

—Luke 5:4–8

Coming to know God is at the same time coming to know myself as "fall[ing] short of the glory of God" (Romans 3:23)—that is, recognizing that God's complete love for me makes me recognize how badly I have loved God in return. Peter's response to Jesus is understandable; he wants Jesus to go away because Jesus' presence makes him hyper-aware of his sin.

Martin Luther King Jr. expressed a profound awareness of the coexistence of pain and healing to be found in acknowledging injustice. In his "Letter from Birmingham Jail" he wrote, "Like a boil that can never be cured so long as it is covered up but must be opened with all its ugliness to the natural medicines of air and light, injustice must be exposed." So, too, with our sin: we must expose it to the light of Christ, the "light of the world" (John 8:12) who brings us healing. That process is difficult but necessary. We may continue to avoid acknowledging sin, moving from one to another and drowning out God's gentle voice, but we will continue to hurt ourselves and others.

In the story above, Jesus comes to Peter and shows him where to find what he is seeking. Peter has been a fisherman all his life; it is likely that he considered himself perfectly competent to make his own decisions about how to do his work. Yet his willingness to trust Jesus leads to an abundance he could not have foreseen. Will my trust in Jesus similarly lead me to new fruitfulness, perhaps of a sort I cannot now see? Will my willingness to name my sin leave a space for God to heal me? And will that healing make me more disposed to do God's work of building a kingdom of justice and mercy?

Prayer

Plan to celebrate the sacrament of reconciliation. Ask God for the healing that God desires to work in you and for the grace to do the work that God wants to accomplish in you by making you more like Christ.

Action

Identify one concrete way to show your love for God as the fruit of reconciliation with God. Beyond whatever formal penance you are assigned (do your Our Fathers or Hail Marys or whatever the priest assigns), undertake one specific act of generous love that orients you toward the building of God's kingdom.

Exercise 7

Repent, and Believe in the Good News

✝

Jesus came to Galilee, proclaiming the good news of God, and saying, "The time is fulfilled, and the kingdom of God has come near; repent, and believe in the good news."

—Mark 1:14–15

The Greek verb *metanoiete*, translated usually as "repent," could just as easily mean "change your minds." Some think of conversion as a kind of magic, as if God randomly chooses people to set aside their brains and believe in strange things. Here, and in the other Gospels, we see Jesus saying something to the effect of "try a new way of looking at things by placing your trust in the Good News I'm sharing with you." In that way, Jesus is less like a magician and more like a professor or journalist who wants to shape the way we look at the world.

The cornerstone of what Jesus wants to share is that God is right here, right now, laboring among us. He labors not as some transcendent other, but rather as a person inviting us to partake in a grand, unfolding project. Jesus' invitation, then, is this: be part of that project, because God needs you to be love where you live. If you aren't that love, who else will do that part of God's project? Who else will agree to be love to your family, your friends, your coworkers, your circle of influence?

Are you willing to set aside your limited perception of the world and allow yourself to learn from

Jesus and the followers of Jesus who have been at it longer than you? Are you willing to participate in a grand, unfolding project of being love for the world, being love for the specific men, women, boys, and girls your life touches? Are you willing to look at all things the way God does and test your understanding against the wisdom of the church? Are you willing to let your life sing to the tune that God conducts, as part of a grand symphony?

Prayer

Bring to prayer your desire to be part of something greater than yourself. Ask God to help you name which specific desires point you in the direction of that "something greater"—God's project—and ask God to bless your attempts to be love for others.

Action

Go to Mass and do an imaginative exercise before it begins. See the people in the congregation as God does, imagining that God has called each person to some specific work in building his kingdom. Imagine that God is calling you, too, to undertake a specific work, and offer yourself in this gathering of the Body of Christ toward God's purposes. Pray with this intention throughout the Mass.

Exercise 8

This Is the Sort of Fast That Pleases Me

†

Is not this the fast that I choose:
to loose the bonds of injustice,
to undo the thongs of the yoke,
to let the oppressed go free,
and to break every yoke?
Is it not to share your bread with the hungry,
and bring the homeless poor into your house;
when you see the naked, to cover them,
and not to hide yourself from your own kin?
Then your light shall break forth like the dawn,
and your healing shall spring up quickly;
your vindicator shall go before you,
the glory of the LORD shall be your rear guard.
Then you shall call, and the LORD will answer;
you shall cry for help, and he will say, Here I am.
—Isaiah 58:6–9

The prophet Isaiah names here what all of us want when we confront our sin, our tendencies to hurt ourselves or others: we desire healing. We desire freedom. We recognize on some level that—in the words of Psalm 51:3—"my sin is ever before me" and that we can't break free through sheer willpower.

Isaiah intimates what it took centuries for theologians to fully understand. Fasting—that is, the willingness to curb a desire the way a farmer prunes a plant—is an act of will to rise from the normal patterns of seeking pleasure and avoiding pain. Such an act of will says yes to God's grace and allows the inrushing of the Holy Spirit, such that God can transform our lives toward holy purposes. This act of openness toward God is possible when we recognize that our attempts to do good are always short of the mark and that only God can effect the healing of our intentions and turn our efforts toward the grand unfolding of a divine project.

When we allow God that space in our lives, our healing will "spring up quickly," and God will emerge from the corners of our minds to take the lead: "your vindicator shall go before you" (Isaiah 58:8).

Prayer

The Jesuit philosopher Bernard Lonergan identified several forms of bias—that is, things that get in the way of our seeing the world as it truly is, as God sees it. Some experiences and convictions skew our understanding of things. Ask God in prayer to help clear your vision so that you can see the world as it truly is. Ask God what desires need to be pruned and how we need to practice fasting so that we may become truly free.

Action

In an earlier time, practices of *mortification* (literally "making death")—that is, small sacrifices to God, such as giving up meat or fasting—were seen as ways to overcome selfishness. After your prayer, consider some form of fasting that is appropriate to your situation: Technology? Coffee? Gossip? Excess sugar? Energy consumption? Name what desire God is asking you to prune as a way of allowing yourself to embrace God's grace more fully.

Exercise 9

Ask, and It Will Be Given to You

†

[Jesus said] "Ask, and it will be given you; search, and you will find; knock, and the door will be opened for you. For everyone who asks receives, and everyone who searches finds, and for everyone who knocks, the door will be opened. Is there anyone among you who, if your child asks for bread, will give a stone? Or if the child asks for a fish, will give a snake? If you then, who are evil, know how to give good gifts to your children, how much more will your Father in heaven give good things to those who ask him!"

—Matthew 7:7–11

The key to this often-misunderstood text lies in the examples that Jesus gives toward the end. As a father, I am very familiar with the dynamic of young children asking for things.

Child: "Can I have a Coke?"

Me: "No, but you can have juice."

Child: "Can you buy me a new toy now?"

Me: "No, but I'll be happy to play a game with you."

Child: "Can you read me a story?"

Me: "Of course!"

The point is that children are always asking for things, and a good parent will often have to say no. But when the child asks for something that a parent knows will benefit the child, the good parent will be delighted to say yes.

So, too, with God; as the one who loves us more than we can understand, God wants to give us gifts—and will often give us gifts that we don't ask for (and maybe don't even understand as worth having). Sometimes these gifts are obvious: a new friendship or a feeling of consolation that comes from loving well. Many times, though, the gifts are obscure or even unwanted: a sting of conscience after sin; difficulty in school or work that points us away from wasting our energies.

Perhaps the most basic act of faith, after believing that God exists, is believing that God is good when evidence seems to point to the contrary. Jesus' words here suggest to us that the God who created us knows our good better than we ever can and that the practice of asking God for gifts is critical to our growing in knowledge of the good to which God is pointing us. We will not always get the object of our asking, but we will in time get what we most truly desire.

Prayer

Make a habit of expressing your desire every day in prayer.

Action

Write down your desires in a journal; return to it over the course of the day. Over time, continue to pay attention to the desires you bring into prayer. Thank God both for prayers answered the way you hope and for prayers answered in ways different from what you expect.

Exercise 10

Be Holy, for I Am Holy

†

You shall be holy, for I the LORD your God am holy. You shall each revere your mother and father, and you shall keep my sabbaths: I am the LORD your God. Do not turn to idols or make cast images for yourselves: I am the LORD your God. . . . You shall not hate in your heart anyone of your kin; you shall reprove your neighbor, or you will incur guilt yourself. You shall not take vengeance or bear a grudge against any of your people, but you shall love your neighbor as yourself: I am the LORD.

—Leviticus 19:2–4, 17–18

The uncomfortable truth about faith—an intimate relationship with God, like a marriage—is that God makes demands. We can't be the same old person we were before we said yes to God's offer of unconditional love. We can't make our response conditional: "I'll have faith as long as I get to . . ." (fill in the blank: "keep this money" or "have this sex" or "ignore what the church has taught" or whatever).

God really makes only one demand, which has myriad implications. God demands holiness. Initially, that may sound terrifying—which one of us can live up to that? For some, that demand may come with images of heaven and hell similar to what medieval artists and writers such as Dante conjured up. But behind that demand is a more fundamental truth: God loves us without condition, with as much generosity when we are horrible sinners as when we are reckless saints. The demand of holiness is most certainly not, then, a condition of God's love for us. It is rather a condition of our happiness.

Imagine wearing expensive clothing and jewelry. You are ready for the cover of *Vogue*. Now imagine entering a sauna—an analogy for entering into the presence of God, whose love is described as a refiner's fire (see Malachi 3:2; 1 Corinthians 3:13). The experience will be torturous for the person concerned with preserving the look, but for the person ready to simply let go of the clothes and makeup, it will be very relaxing. God's demand for holiness is ultimately a demand that we let go of what prevents us from taking comfort in the presence of God.

The challenge, of course, is that many things get in the way of our taking comfort. The author of Leviticus names several, but in our own day there are many more. Through our participation in the life of the church, we come to better awareness of these obstacles so that we might let go of them.

Prayer

Pray for the grace to understand what is getting in the way of holiness. Ask God to help you name and let go of the false desires that lead you to cling to any obstacle to holiness.

Action

Learn about the life of a modern saint, and pay attention to what he or she had to overcome in order to become free to follow Christ.

Second

Christ Calls Me to Service

Help me to become more like Jesus so that I may live in freedom to do God's loving work.

Exercise 11

The Sick Need a Doctor

†

As [Jesus] sat at dinner in the house, many tax collectors and sinners came and were sitting with him and his disciples. When the Pharisees saw this, they said to his disciples, "Why does your teacher eat with tax collectors and sinners?" But when he heard this, he said, "Those who are well have no need of a physician, but those who are sick. Go and learn what this means, 'I desire mercy, not sacrifice.' For I have come to call not the righteous but sinners."

—Matthew 9:10–13

Throughout his Gospel, Matthew writes for his fellow Jews who were surprised and sometimes scandalized by the way Jesus went about his ministry. Here, he describes one of many scenes when Jesus challenges the Pharisees' misunderstanding of what God desires.

The Pharisees held closely to the holiness code in the book of Leviticus, a portion of which we saw in Exercise 10. Their understanding of holiness stressed the idea that to be like God is to be set apart, healed of sin and therefore unlike others who keep falling into sin. Jesus takes another approach, stressing that holiness is like the health a person gains after being in a hospital, but only if God's servants go out to bring the sick in on stretchers. (A similar image appears in John chapter 5, where a sick man complains of wanting to reach the healing waters of Bethesda but has no one to carry him there.)

Our desire to be more like Jesus means being willing to be one of those servants. It means we will be hanging around hospitals (either literal or metaphorical ones) often. First, it means being willing to seek Christ's healing—accepting Christ's dealing with our own sin and unwellness. Second, it means being willing to work at maintaining our spiritual health by avoiding sin. Third, it means constantly asking God where he would send us to bring the sick to him, the divine Physician, so that he might show mercy.

Prayer

Begin to make a habit of the *examen*, a prayer of reflection, over the course of the day, with an eye to better understanding where God is moving you.[4] As you look over the day, where do you feel God's love most strongly? Where do you feel the stirrings of desire? Where do you feel sadness over sin? Bring all these movements into conversation with God, asking him to show you where he is sending you to help bring healing.

Action

Read one of the Gospels the whole way through, and pay close attention to how Jesus is portrayed. Each Evangelist gives a somewhat different portrayal of who Jesus is. Learn to note what each author stresses and get to know Jesus as a person. Take your time—maybe a chapter or two a day. Read it not with the hungry eyes that seek information, as with social media, but with meditative eyes.

---

4. For help in learning how to pray the Examen, see
   www.ignatianspirituality.com/ignatian-prayer/the-examen/.

Exercise 12

Come and See

†

John again was standing with two of his disciples, and as he watched Jesus walk by, he exclaimed, "Look, here is the Lamb of God!" The two disciples heard him say this, and they followed Jesus. When Jesus turned and saw them following, he said to them, "What are you looking for?" They said to him, "Rabbi" (which translated means Teacher), "where are you staying?" He said to them, "Come and see." They came and saw where he was staying, and they remained with him that day.

—John 1:35–39

Putting aside for a moment the technical term "Lamb of God"—a reference that first-century Jews would have understood as referring to the Passover celebration—let's observe that what happens in this story is a teacher directing his students to someone he knows to be a greater teacher than himself. In their curiosity, they go after Jesus and accept his invitation to get to know him better.

John's role of pointing his students to Jesus is the role of every Christian, called to share the good news of what Jesus has done. And Jesus' invitation to John's students is the same for everyone: come and see for yourself what I'm about. Don't just rely on what other people tell you.

Today, Christianity has a long history, meaning that centuries of rituals, doctrines, moral teachings, historical events, successes, and missteps can obscure the kind of primary encounter with Jesus that John exhorts his students to seek. Yet that exhortation has not changed: learn for yourself. Don't let what you've read or heard or seen get in the way. Everyone has a limited and biased understanding of the church and of Jesus. In the Internet age especially, all of us are likely to encounter perspectives that more or less resonate with our own: we have favorite news sites, social media, and habits of browsing. We tend to associate with like-minded people. And so our understanding of Jesus and his church is likely to be influenced in large part by the teachers we rely on—whether they are reputable or not, whether they are accredited or not, whether they have authority or not.

John's great wisdom is to say to his students, in effect, "Don't take my word for it. Go talk to him yourself." For us, that means prayer.

Prayer

As you read the Gospels, give yourself time to speak to the Jesus you encounter. Enter the stories; sit with them; imagine yourself in them, conversing with Jesus. What are you feeling?

Action

After your prayer, identify one action over the course of the coming day by which you can imitate the Jesus you are discovering in the Gospels. Ask yourself how Jesus might act in the situation. Consider what elements of his approach (generosity, spontaneity, willingness to take risks, compassion even when it meant others' disapproval, and so on) might influence your approach. Be willing to take the risk of seeing "where he stays"—that is, how he chose to look at the world and his role in it.

Exercise 13

Glad Tidings to the Poor

✝

When [Jesus] came to Nazareth, where he had been brought up, he went to the synagogue on the sabbath day, as was his custom. He stood up to read, and the scroll of the prophet Isaiah was given to him. He unrolled the scroll and found the place where it was written:

> *"The Spirit of the Lord is upon me,*
> > *because he has anointed me to bring good news to*
> > > *the poor.*
> *He has sent me to proclaim release to the captives*
> > *and recovery of sight to the blind, to let the*
> > > *oppressed go free,*
> *to proclaim the year of the Lord's favor."*

—Luke 4:16–19

Every true Christian vocation is a vocation to serve those who are poor, in need, marginalized. Our challenge is to discern how God calls us—that is, to understand which people most need the unique gifts with which God has endowed us for the sake of service.

Our Catholic tradition names several categories of service, known as the corporal and spiritual works of mercy.

The corporal works of mercy are

- feeding the hungry
- giving drink to the thirsty
- clothing the naked
- sheltering the homeless
- visiting the sick
- visiting the imprisoned
- burying the dead

The spiritual works of mercy are

- admonishing the sinner
- instructing the ignorant

- counseling the doubtful
- comforting the sorrowful
- bearing wrongs patiently
- forgiving all injuries
- praying for the living and the dead

What is clear from the Gospels is that Jesus moved with purpose in his ministry: teaching and healing; reaching out to those on the margins and challenging those with power; calling people to repent of their sins and prepare for God's mercy and judgment. He undertook a ministry to the poor—both those without money and those without knowledge of God. Perhaps most important, he did these things with no particular concern for himself. In a word, he was free. He abandoned himself to God's grace, approached death with equanimity, and then showed that God could overcome death itself.

Prayer

During this second week, make your prayer "Help me be more like Jesus." Put yourself into the Gospel stories, and imagine yourself taking part. What do you hear as you listen to Jesus? What do you see as others listen to him? What might it be like to be Jesus yourself? Give yourself the chance to use all your senses to make the scenes vivid, and write down your responses afterward.

Action

Make some specific commitment to manifest your desire to be like Jesus. Perhaps it will mean wearing a cross or posting something about your faith on social media. Pay attention to the reactions you get: some positive, some negative—just like the reactions Jesus received. Simply acknowledge the reactions and bring them into prayer, as Jesus did.

Exercise 14

Washing Feet

✝

Jesus, knowing that the Father had given all things into his hands, and that he had come from God and was going to God, got up from the table, took off his outer robe, and tied a towel around himself. Then he poured water into a basin and began to wash the disciples' feet and to wipe them with the towel that was tied around him. He came to Simon Peter, who said to him, "Lord, are you going to wash my feet?" Jesus answered, "You do not know now what I am doing, but later you will understand." Peter said to him, "You will never wash my feet." Jesus answered, "Unless I wash you, you have no share with me."

—John 13:3–8

There are two elements in this story that are surprising. The first is that Jesus does something as humble as washing feet. The second is that he basically tells us that we have to do the same thing. His example is challenging—saying, in essence, that the normal boundaries don't apply when it comes to following him. Don't worry about your image, he seems to be saying—worry instead about being part of what I am doing.

Jesus is calling us to freedom from the hang-ups that prevent us from giving ourselves fully to love. "The kingdom of heaven is right here!" he says in so many words—right in the people around you now—and the only inhibitions to embracing it fully are our fears.

In his famous prayer known as the *Suscipe,* St. Ignatius begins with the line "Take, O Lord, and receive . . . my memory." I once found this a curious beginning to a prayer, but now I understand it to mean that we hope God will transform the self-understanding we have gained over our lives so that we remember ourselves differently. For by giving our memory to God, we release our hold on the limited self-image or "reputation" we have built and enter freely into loving service to the world. My past no longer limits me; I am here to serve, to wash the world's feet.

Prayer

As you continue to read the Gospel, pay attention to what feelings stir in you. When you pay attention to what Jesus says and does, are you surprised? Overjoyed? Angry? Frustrated? Be honest and note these stirrings in a journal, and bring them into prayer. Which stories are staying with you during the day? Return in prayer to a story that elicits the strongest feelings from you, and ask God how you are to understand it in the concrete situation of your life right now. Write about your experiences.

Action

Take a look at your past week or month, and pay attention to the times you were in direct service to another person—a family member or someone else close to you (a neighbor, friend, coworker, or classmate) or a complete stranger. Take note of the feelings that such service elicits, good or bad.

Remember that not all service is wholly good. Parents, for example, know that sometimes children can take advantage of service; spouses and friends know that service can collapse into being manipulated. What does my seeking the good in service really demand?

Exercise 15

Let the Party Continue

✝

There was a wedding in Cana of Galilee. . . . When the wine gave out, the mother of Jesus said to him, "They have no wine." And Jesus said to her, "Woman, what concern is that to you and to me? My hour has not yet come." His mother said to the servants, "Do whatever he tells you." Now standing there were six stone water jars for the Jewish rites of purification, each holding twenty or thirty gallons. Jesus said to them, "Fill the jars with water." And they filled them up to the brim. He said to them, "Now draw some out, and take it to the chief steward." So they took it. When the steward tasted the water that had become wine, and did not know where it came from (though the servants who had drawn the water knew), the steward called the bridegroom and said to him, "Everyone serves the good wine first, and then the inferior wine after the guests have become drunk. But you have kept the good wine until now." Jesus did this, the first of his signs, in Cana of Galilee, and revealed his glory; and his disciples believed in him.

—John 2:1, 3–11

In John's Gospel, Jesus begins his public ministry with the miracle of changing water into wine. Why does he choose this action, rather than something more—well—Godlike? Why not raise someone from the dead or heal some people—or for that matter, cure cancer, eliminate poverty, and end war? Why do a miracle that simply allows a party to continue?

There is something intensely paradoxical about this first miracle that should give us pause in our efforts to change the world. Jesus' actions are always personal and always surprising. He was not a social-justice crusader. At no point did Jesus challenge the oppressive Roman government, organize the poor to demand their rights, or lead a boycott against the religious authorities. He simply wanted to reveal God's glory and to show that he himself was the bearer of it. He was fabulously unconcerned with applying divine power to scare people. His actions were rather modest and even capricious, in this case, simply obeying his mom's directions to help out an impecunious bridegroom.

This week, as you contemplate Jesus' invitation to "come and see" who he is and what he's about, pay attention both to what he does and does not do. Why does he show his power? What are the conditions that allow him to work miracles? What seems to be his objective? This is not a man who appears to be on a massive public relations campaign, announcing the presence of God in a carefully strategized sequence. He seems much more interested in random acts of compassion that get him into trouble.

Prayer

Ask Jesus to teach you how to walk with him and be his presence in the world. Ask his Holy Spirit to guide you to acts of compassion like those he revealed in unexpected places. Open your eyes and look for those opportunities.

Action

Choose one concrete way to express compassion today.

Exercise 16

Blessed Are You

†

[Jesus] looked up at his disciples and said:
"Blessed are you who are poor,
for yours is the kingdom of God.
Blessed are you who are hungry now,
for you will be filled.
Blessed are you who weep now,
for you will laugh.
Blessed are you when people hate you, and when they
exclude you, revile you, and defame you on account
of the Son of Man. Rejoice in that day and leap for
joy, for surely your reward is great in heaven; for that
is what their ancestors did to the prophets."

—Luke 6:20–23

The Beatitudes are an insider's guide to the Christian life, inasmuch as they describe what it's like to be on mission in the world. Every customary marker of success, Jesus suggests, is wrong—and what appears to be difficult may in fact be a sign of fidelity to building God's kingdom.

I imagine what it might be like to be part of a great team embarking on a hoped-for championship season. The coach tells the team members of the hardships they will face, the struggles they will have to overcome in order to achieve victory. A good coach will be honest about what the team members must face so that they will not lose heart when, inevitably, things don't always go as hoped.

In the Beatitudes, Christ takes a similar approach, suggesting that the distant hope for building the kingdom will involve highs and lows. He tells his students that this mission will be arduous but that the reward will be heaven itself.

You'll know that you're building God's kingdom, Jesus says, when people "hate you, and when they exclude you, revile you, and defame you" (Luke 6:22), just as people did to the prophets.

People hate those sent by God because such people always sting the consciences of the self-righteous. Jesus upset things through his outreach to lepers, to women, and to tax collectors and sinners. Today, Christians sting consciences through outreach to the poor, children yet to be born, immigrants and refugees, families, the sick, and many others.

Whose good is Christ calling you to serve? Are you willing to be reviled for the work to which Christ has called you? Are you willing to take a stand on behalf of those who have not the power to stand for themselves, and work tirelessly in the face of harassment? If so, Jesus says, you are blessed.

Prayer

Bring before God your desires to love and serve those he has given you the talent and inclination to serve.

Action

Ask God to show you the ways that the church has sought to reach out to those beloved children of God, and learn from them. It might mean reading from the wisdom of the church's teachings or volunteering at an organization that provides outreach in Jesus' name.

Exercise 17

Calming the Storm

✝

When [Jesus] got into the boat, his disciples followed him. A windstorm arose on the sea, so great that the boat was being swamped by the waves; but he was asleep. And they went and woke him up, saying, "Lord, save us! We are perishing!" And he said to them, "Why are you afraid, you of little faith?" Then he got up and rebuked the winds and the sea; and there was a dead calm. They were amazed, saying, "What sort of man is this, that even the winds and the sea obey him?"

—Matthew 8:23–27

The story of Jesus calming the storm reads as a kind of metaphor for the life of mission, saying, in effect, "Don't worry about how bad things get as long as you are close to the Lord." In Matthew's Gospel, the story comes after the Sermon on the Mount (where he delivered the Beatitudes, as in Exercise 16). Jesus has performed some healings and called new disciples. He is a man on a mission, and his students are just trying to keep up. Everything about their life with Jesus is startling—they are like children who are with their father during "come to work" day. Something happens! They don't know what to do! Carrying the metaphor a step further, it is as if a phone rings in the office, and they, never having heard a phone before, get scared. "Dad! Dad! There's a loud noise!"

Jesus is completely unconcerned about what appears to be a problem to the disciples. We recall the words of the Beatitudes: "Blessed are you when people hate you, and when they exclude you, revile you, and defame you on account of the Son of Man" (Luke 6:22). For many of us, the negative and at times hateful reactions of people around us can lead to depression or self-loathing. Jesus upends our concerns: "Why are you afraid, you of little faith?" (Matthew 8:26). Of course there are problems we must face; they are the birth pangs that presage the coming of the kingdom (see Matthew 24:3–35). The enemy of our nature wants to dissuade us from carrying on in the face of these storms. Jesus' response is to see through those lies, as he did when the devil tempted him (see Matthew 4:1–11), keeping his eyes on the ministry with which the Father has entrusted him. We must do the same.

Prayer

Speak to God of the storms in your life: the experiences that make it difficult to remain faithful to the call Jesus has given you. Bring what is secret before Jesus and ask him to drive the storms away.

Action

Use an experience of a "storm" as an opportunity to give thanks to God. Become aware of your natural desire to react negatively, to lash out in anger or hurt. Take time to invite God into the experience, and see it the way Jesus saw the storm.

Exercise 18

Feeding Five Thousand

†

The day was drawing to a close, and the twelve came to him and said, "Send the crowd away, so that they may go into the surrounding villages and countryside, to lodge and get provisions; for we are here in a deserted place." But he said to them, "You give them something to eat." They said, "We have no more than five loaves and two fish—unless we are to go and buy food for all these people." For there were about five thousand men. And he said to his disciples, "Make them sit down in groups of about fifty each." They did so and made them all sit down. And taking the five loaves and the two fish, he looked up to heaven, and blessed and broke them, and gave them to the disciples to set before the crowd. And all ate and were filled. What was left over was gathered up, twelve baskets of broken pieces.

—Luke 9:12–17

I have always found Jesus' words to the disciples here the most puzzling: "You give them something to eat" (Luke 9:13). Why does he say this, knowing they have no resources, then turn around and perform a miracle?

I think the story is a clue to the way God works. He is not a passive gift-giver, like a rich father spoiling his children. He wants his children to act, to be poised with desire to bring about the kingdom.

In the introduction to this book, I suggested that there is a balance to our action and God's action. We don't earn salvation by our actions, but neither do we sit passively and allow God to do all the work. Jesus' words here are critical; he wants the disciples to do something, even if it is simply to express the desire that they hope to see fulfilled. We must do the same in prayer, bringing before the Lord what we hope to see him accomplish, as we saw in Exercise 9. Perhaps what our action does is express in freedom the desire that God act—opening, as it were, the door to God's abundant love.

Prayer

Express your desire to Jesus: tell him what you want to happen. Do this every day, and attend to what emerges in your consciousness over time. Are your desires becoming more specific, less like "save the world" and more like "help me make a difference in this child's life"? Does your expression of desire help you discern the way that God is leading you to participate in the building of his kingdom?

Action

Take a look at your daily life, and pay attention to acts of direct service to others. What is the deep desire that animates these daily acts of service? Write in a journal about what deep desire you hope will find fruition as you cooperate with God to create yourself anew. Learn about the ministries of the church to which you might contribute by cultivating this deep desire. Go online and study what different Catholic religious orders, schools, universities, social services, and organizations are doing. Where do you feel called?

Exercise 19

Not in This House

†

In the temple [Jesus] found people selling cattle, sheep, and doves, and the money changers seated at their tables. Making a whip of cords, he drove all of them out of the temple, both the sheep and the cattle. He also poured out the coins of the money changers and overturned their tables. He told those who were selling the doves, "Take these things out of here! Stop making my Father's house a marketplace!"

—John 2:14–16

Imagine, if you can, what our use of money might look like if there were no sin. We would use it for the sake of trade and to encourage creative work that served the common good. We would not see harmful risk-taking of the sort that we find in, say, casinos or stock markets. We would not see employers making many times the amount they pay workers. We would not see the fleecing of customers, the powerful preying on the vulnerable, and rapacious lending.

We also would not see so much of the competition that characterizes modern life. Children and adults seeking education would see their fellow students as co-learners, helping to build the world. Businesspeople would not see others as competitors but rather as collaborators. Advertisers would see themselves as information sharers and would avoid the exploitation of people through constant exposure to sexual themes and inflated false desires. Entrepreneurs and those with many resources would create opportunities for people to secure decent lives for themselves and their families.

Many read Jesus' action in the temple as a criticism of the way the money changers were profaning a sacred space. There is another way to understand this action, though. The world is God's house, and every misuse of money is a violation of God's command to love my neighbor as myself. In this respect, money is no different from any other of the tools people use, except perhaps in the frequency with which we use it. Jesus' criticism points to the ways that people tend to act differently in the sacred space (the temple), which ought to mirror life in God's kingdom, from the places "outside the temple" (in Latin, *pro fanum*). Many are tempted to use money not for the sake of building the kingdom, but to become (in the words of St. Augustine) "turned inward on themselves" (*incurvatus in se*). Like the child holding his thumb up to block the sun, our sinful attitude toward money prevents us from seeing the great good that Christ is trying to work in us.

Prayer

Ask the Holy Spirit to shine light on the places where you present obstacles to grace. Ask for the grace to know in particular how you use and think about money. Ask how your attitudes might be turned toward greater building of God's kingdom.

Action

Make a substantial commitment to use money for the sake of the kingdom. Build that commitment into your daily life; your monthly bills; your annual budget.

Exercise 20

Seeing Jesus in a New Way

†

Jesus took with him Peter and James and his brother John and led them up a high mountain, by themselves. And he was transfigured before them, and his face shone like the sun, and his clothes became dazzling white. Suddenly there appeared to them Moses and Elijah, talking with him. Then Peter said to Jesus, "Lord, it is good for us to be here; if you wish, I will make three dwellings here, one for you, one for Moses, and one for Elijah." While he was still speaking, suddenly a bright cloud overshadowed them, and from the cloud a voice said, "This is my Son, the Beloved; with him I am well pleased; listen to him!" When the disciples heard this, they fell to the ground and were overcome by fear. But Jesus came and touched them, saying, "Get up and do not be afraid."

—Matthew 17:1–7

Throughout the Gospels, we see Jesus taking Peter and some other disciples aside to share with them more intimate moments, teaching them things he does not share with the many others who are curious to see what he is about. Jesus is like all of us: we don't usually broadcast the details of our lives to everyone, and even when we do—as on social media or reality TV shows—the sheer volume of information makes it unlikely that most people will really care.

In the story of the Transfiguration, we see Jesus with his closest friends, his inner circle—the men whom he relied on most. This is not the public Jesus: the charismatic rabbi, the healer, the wonder worker. Jesus' public face is real, but Jesus the intimate friend is more than the sum of his public words and actions. What Peter, James, and John see is Jesus up close, real, and personal, and they are awestruck. Peter would write of this event later:

> He received honor and glory from God the Father when that voice was conveyed to him by the Majestic Glory, saying, "This is my Son, my Beloved, with whom I am well pleased." We ourselves heard

this voice come from heaven, while we were with him on the holy mountain. (2 Peter 1:17–18)

Peter is stunned to have this kind of intimate knowledge of Jesus. Knowing Jesus, he begins to know God face-to-face, and he is forever changed.

We are tempted to believe sometimes that religion or spirituality is about ideas, abstractions, words, texts, principles, moral teachings, beliefs, doctrines, or philosophical systems. But here the Gospel tells a basic truth: our faith is about coming to know a *person*: faith involves being invited into intimacy with Jesus. We need ideas, belief systems, and the rest, but in the end we must simply allow Jesus to reveal himself to us, allow his heart to speak to our heart, so that we, too, might behold his glory.

Prayer

Find an icon of the face of Christ and allow your gaze on that image to move you past words, to allow Jesus' heart to speak to your heart.

Action

Practice using your imagination to see the face of Christ in the people you meet today. How does seeing Christ transform the way you interact with people?

Third

I Hurt Because I Love

I don't want those I love to suffer alone.

Exercise 21

Triumphal Entry

†

The disciples went and did as Jesus had directed them; they brought the donkey and the colt, and put their cloaks on them, and he sat on them. A very large crowd spread their cloaks on the road, and others cut branches from the trees and spread them on the road. The crowds that went ahead of him and that followed were shouting, "Hosanna to the Son of David! Blessed is the one who comes in the name of the Lord! Hosanna in the highest heaven!"

—Matthew 21:6–9

One day, crowds gather and welcome a celebrity into their midst. Another day, they watch him get tortured and killed. What is going on here?

Jesus is completely unconcerned with the adulation of the crowds, in this situation and others. Like any modern story of the celebrity who is lionized one day and vilified the next, this one points to the unreliability of public opinion as a barometer of divine favor. The "voice of the people" may sometimes be the voice of God, but if so, it's coincidence. God often directs his servants to expose personal and social sins: biblical figures such as Noah, Moses, the prophets, Jesus, Paul, and the disciples; saints such as Augustine, Francis of Assisi, Catherine of Siena, and Bartolomé de las Casas; latter-day figures such as Martin Luther King Jr., Óscar Romero, Mother Teresa, Sr. Helen Prejean, and Pope John Paul II.

We who have fragile egos so often act in light of what we perceive to be the voice of the people. It is very difficult to hold truths that are frowned upon by those around us, especially difficult moral or political issues that are constantly in the news. Jesus' example here shows us that the right action is never based on looking around us at what others think; it is always about obeying God's commands. And following God's commands—as Jesus did—may lead us into conflict.

We practice discernment of God's commands by remaining close to Christ and Christ's Body, the church. In doing so, we place ourselves with the poor, the suffering, the forgotten, the abused, and the hated: God's beloved creatures whom others have forgotten. We choose to see humanity where others see problems: the child starving on the streets or growing in her destitute mother's womb; the young prostitute whose daily bread comes from the grasping hands of sex tourists; the foster child shuttled from home to home; the elderly person in need of health care. Seeing Jesus in those people, we ask three simple questions: what have I done for Jesus? What am I doing for Jesus? What will I do for Jesus?

Prayer

Lord, you are intimately present in every part of your creation. Help me see your face in every person—those people I see daily and those whose lives touch mine because of our interconnected world. Grant me a discerning heart so that I can work with you to make my life a sign of your kingdom always coming forth. Help me understand the biases that prevent me from seeing you. Help me understand the social mores and structures that get in the way of your justice and mercy. Help me remain unconcerned with the praise of others, but always keep my eyes on the good you are bringing forth in my life.

Action

Build into your daily or weekly reading critical commentary from members of the church on difficult contemporary issues. Bookmark websites; look for people and organizations to follow on social media. Develop habits to cultivate thinking and feeling with the church. Practice seeing the world the way God does, regardless of whether or not it's currently popular. Avoid forming opinions based on surveys.

Exercise 22

Foot Washing

†

Now before the festival of the Passover, Jesus knew that his hour had come to depart from this world and go to the Father. Having loved his own who were in the world, he loved them to the end. The devil had already put it into the heart of Judas son of Simon Iscariot to betray him. And during supper, Jesus, knowing that the Father had given all things into his hands, and that he had come from God and was going to God, got up from the table, took off his outer robe, and tied a towel around himself. Then he poured water into a basin and began to wash the disciples' feet and to wipe them with the towel that was tied around him. . . . After he had washed their feet, had put on his robe, and had returned to the table, he said to them, "Do you know what I have done to you? You call me Teacher and Lord—and you are right, for that is what I am. So if I, your Lord and Teacher, have washed your feet, you also ought to wash one another's feet. For I have set you an example, that you also should do as I have done to you."

—John 13:1–5, 12–15

John's account of the foot washing—unique among the Gospels—is one of the clearest directions about how to be a follower of Jesus. It is hard to miss the symbolism here: washing others' feet means being in a humble position of service.

One of the most striking actions in the early pontificate of Pope Francis was his decision to wash the feet of several inmates at a juvenile detention center. "I must be at your service," he said. He took Jesus' command quite literally but also used the opportunity to offer a comment on what it means to be of service: to be ready to find those who are at the margins in order to manifest Christlike love. Usually, the foot washing ceremony, performed on Holy Thursday, is done in a church with members of the community. Francis used this old practice to recall for us that Christ's mission was not primarily in the temple; it was out in the world, among lepers and prostitutes and tax collectors.

Jesus' action was performed among the twelve he had chosen to be his closest associates—those who would carry his mission to the rest of the world. Yet it took place on the eve of his most public humiliation, his arrest and crucifixion. There is a "missionary" dimension to Jesus' foot washing, a kind of alter-baptism. He washes the feet of those he is sending out into the world to continue the work he has begun, preaching the good news of God's love, manifest in Jesus' own willingness to suffer death for the sake of the world's salvation. Will you join in that mission? Will you let Jesus wash your feet? And will you wash the feet of others?

Prayer

Imagine that Jesus is washing your feet. Are your feet tired from walking all day? Hot and gritty, full of aches and pains? Imagine how it feels for Jesus to hold your feet, the relief of the clean water, the comfort of the towel. What emotions are you feeling? Do you say anything to Jesus while this is happening? When your eyes meet his, what do you see?

Action

If you are a caregiver (perhaps of a child or elderly person), use an opportunity when you are in physical contact with him or her to be an opportunity for prayer. Maybe you do actually wash feet or hands; if so, ask God to bless your hands. If you do not have such an opportunity, seek out a volunteer opportunity that allows you to use your hands to lovingly serve another. Notice the way that using your body in service to another brings attentiveness to your prayer.

Exercise 23

Last Supper

✝

For I received from the Lord what I also handed on to you, that the Lord Jesus on the night when he was betrayed took a loaf of bread, and when he had given thanks, he broke it and said, "This is my body that is for you. Do this in remembrance of me." In the same way he took the cup also, after supper, saying, "This cup is the new covenant in my blood. Do this, as often as you drink it, in remembrance of me." For as often as you eat this bread and drink the cup, you proclaim the Lord's death until he comes.

—1 Corinthians 11:23–26

Paul's account of the Last Supper is the first that we know to have been written. It reflects the outline of the story that the Evangelists later flesh out in their accounts; it also reflects a basic understanding that the earliest Christians came to hold. "For as often as you eat this bread and drink the cup, you proclaim the Lord's death until he comes" (1 Corinthians 11:26). There is a note of urgency in Paul's language, echoing so much of his other writings: we must tell this story. We must gather together to share the bread and the cup so that others may know of Christ's death and what it means.

Yet at the beginning, the disciples were unsure of what Jesus meant with his action. Imagine their incredulity at Jesus' words at the Last Supper. Luke, a companion of Paul, described Jesus as saying, "This cup that is poured out for you is the new covenant in my blood" (Luke 22:20). Surely the disciples would have recognized his reference to the old covenant, sealed by the blood of the lambs sacrificed to recall the Passover of the Lord in Egypt. But did he mean that they, too, were to be part of the sacrifice? Or rather that he was a *new* lamb of God, and that they would be led to freedom because of his sacrifice?

The disciples' huddling in the upper room after Jesus' death was not at first a sign of evangelical ardor, but rather of fear that something terrible was going to happen to them as it had happened to Jesus. It is important to recall that the earliest Christians were not divine soldiers going to conquer the world; they were confused men and women trying to figure out what exactly Jesus meant. Only later, after his resurrection and the gift of the Holy Spirit at Pentecost, did the full meaning of their experiences become clear.

It is good to remember this pattern in our own lives. Living in faith is not living always in certainty; more often it is living in trust that whatever suffering we undertake out of love for following Jesus will become clear to us eventually. God loves us and includes us in his work in the world.

Prayer

At Mass, put yourself in the place of the disciples. Imagine Jesus speaking the words of the Eucharist to you. Can you trust him? What does it feel like to trust Jesus with your life, your actions, and your future? Bring these emotions into your prayer conversation with him.

Action

Spend time in adoration of the Blessed Sacrament. Use the opportunity to consider how Jesus calls you to "proclaim the Lord's death until he comes."

Exercise 24

Agony in the Garden

✝

[Jesus] withdrew from them about a stone's throw, knelt down, and prayed, "Father, if you are willing, remove this cup from me; yet, not my will but yours be done." Then an angel from heaven appeared to him and gave him strength. In his anguish he prayed more earnestly, and his sweat became like great drops of blood falling down on the ground. When he got up from prayer, he came to the disciples and found them sleeping because of grief.

—Luke 22:41–45

For each of us, there comes a time when the certainties that have guided us in the past are unable to sustain us during crisis. What is remarkable about the synoptic Gospels is their inclusion of such a time in the life of Jesus, in the Garden of Gethsemane. He is fully aware of the mission the Father has entrusted to him: he heals the blind and the lame; he preaches the coming of the kingdom; he raises the dead to life; he predicts his own death. Yet in the garden, Jesus finds himself plunged into grief—a swelling, overwhelming fear that drowns whatever intellectual assent he has given to the Father's will. He *knows* that the Father has called him to witness to faith; he *knows* that there is resurrection from the dead; he *knows* that he is held in the loving embrace of the Father, even unto death; and yet he *feels* terrified.

There is a deep wisdom in feeling: a pre-rational, pre-intellectual grasp of the reality of things. The scientifically minded might point to the residue of our evolutionary past, perhaps recognizing that the limbic system (which governs the fight-or-flight instincts) has a hold on us otherwise rational creatures. What the perfectly human Jesus shows us is that such an experience of being overwhelmed is not antithetical to the life of faith; it can happen even in the climactic unfolding of it. Jesus is about to go to the cross and die and be raised again to new life, and yet he is having a crisis of faith. This is good news, even though it is difficult good news—for we, too, who live by faith, will face times of terror and uncertainty.

The temptation that Jesus faces is very real: will he love to the very end? Will he allow the Father to choose for him what must be done, even though he himself feels that there must be another way? Will he allow the logic of love to take its full course rather than a detour that allows him relief in the short term? Will he allow the Father to reveal his love right in the midst of agonizing suffering?

Prayer

Meditate on a period of suffering in your own life. If you are in the midst of it now, make Jesus' prayer your own: "Remove this cup from me; yet, not my will but yours be done." What feelings stir in you as you consider these words?

If this is a time not of suffering but of consolation, recall a past experience of desolation and recognize that others will happen in the future. What have you learned from your past? What do you want to say to God?

Action

Reach out in a concrete way to someone you know who is experiencing desolation. Cook dinner; send a card; offer prayers. Recall that the disciples were asleep when Jesus endured his desolate time of trial and temptation.

Exercise 25

Arrest

†

Immediately, while [Jesus] was still speaking, Judas, one of the twelve, arrived; and with him there was a crowd with swords and clubs, from the chief priests, the scribes, and the elders. Now the betrayer had given them a sign, saying, "The one I will kiss is the man; arrest him and lead him away under guard." So when he came, he went up to him at once and said, "Rabbi!" and kissed him. Then they laid hands on him and arrested him. But one of those who stood near drew his sword and struck the slave of the high priest, cutting off his ear. Then Jesus said to them, "Have you come out with swords and clubs to arrest me as though I were a bandit? Day after day I was with you in the temple teaching, and you did not arrest me. But let the scriptures be fulfilled." All of them deserted him and fled.

—Mark 14:43–50

The follower of Christ will, if he or she remains faithful, face suffering. The reason is simple: people are prone to sin, and in any institution sin is magnified. Jesus' own life testifies to this simple truth. He preached the kingdom; he showed merciful, compassionate love to those on the margins of society; he challenged the religious and political leaders of the time, and they sought to kill him.

The sad story of Judas offers us a window into the effect of sin. Here is a man who knew Jesus intimately, and who—whether out of ignorance or malice, it is impossible to say—chose to act against him. Perhaps he was simply a feckless pawn who, impatient with Jesus' humility, hoped to move Jesus to a position of political activism. Perhaps he wanted a stronger demonstration of Jesus' power by drawing him into a public demonstration against Rome. Perhaps he believed Jesus was a fake. In any case, Judas's sin against Jesus is caught up in the larger machinations of power among the religious and political leadership of the region, and Jesus is arrested. The Son of God is thrown into prison.

What is astounding is that Jesus offers almost no defense. Why does he not call Herod or Pontius Pilate on their injustices? Why does he not use the opportunity to stand before the Sanhedrin to denounce their perversion of justice? Why does he go quietly? What is he trying to avoid? And where is God the Father in all this?

Prayer

Lord, you let your only Son be led by unjust men to jail, and you let him suffer. I do not understand my suffering or the sufferings of others; I do not understand the injustices of the world. Yet I trust that you are with us when we suffer, and that your will unfolds even where there is great suffering. Stay with me in my suffering, and help me to be present in your name to others who suffer. I do not ask for understanding of suffering, only your grace in the midst of it.

Action

Learn about programs that minister to people in prison. Consider how you might participate in such a ministry or otherwise support it.

Exercise 26

Trial

†

As soon as it was morning, the chief priests held a consultation with the elders and scribes and the whole council. They bound Jesus, led him away, and handed him over to Pilate. Pilate asked him, "Are you the King of the Jews?" He answered him, "You say so." Then the chief priests accused him of many things. Pilate asked him again, "Have you no answer? See how many charges they bring against you." But Jesus made no further reply, so that Pilate was amazed.

Now at the festival he used to release a prisoner for them, anyone for whom they asked. Now a man called Barabbas was in prison with the rebels who had committed murder during the insurrection. So the crowd came and began to ask Pilate to do for them according to his custom. Then he answered them, "Do you want me to release for you the King of the Jews?" For he realized that it was out of jealousy that the chief priests had handed him over. But the chief priests stirred up the crowd to have him release Barabbas for them instead. Pilate spoke to them again, "Then what do you wish me to do with the man you call the King of the Jews?" They shouted back, "Crucify him!" Pilate asked them, "Why, what evil has he done?" But they shouted all the more, "Crucify him!" So Pilate, wishing to satisfy the crowd, released Barabbas for them; and after flogging Jesus, he handed him over to be crucified.

—Mark 15:1–15

The scene of Jesus' trial is in stark contrast to the earlier scene of his agony in the garden. Here, Jesus appears resigned, even indifferent: there is none of the terror he showed earlier. Paradoxically, we see no reference to the Father, whose apparent absence from the scene is striking. Why does it seem to us that in our times of great need God can be deafeningly silent?

In his meditation on suffering, St. John of the Cross described the necessity of the "dark night of the soul," the feeling of God's absence:

> it is fitting that, if the understanding is to be united with that light and become Divine in the state of perfection, it should first of all be purged and annihilated as to its natural light, and, by means of this dark contemplation, be brought actually into darkness. This darkness should continue for as long as is needful in order to expel and annihilate the habit which the soul has long since formed in its manner of understanding, and the Divine light and illumination will then take its place. (*Dark Night of the Soul*, IX.3)

What Jesus shows in his experience of trial is readiness to do what he knows the Father has asked of him, even to go to a painful death. This is Jesus' own paradigmatic act of faith: to trust the Father up to his death, even when the Father seems absent.

Prayer

What does a meditative reading of the story of the trial stir up in you? What trials have you faced, or are you facing? Can you find a place in your heart where you are willing to trust God the way Jesus did?

Action

In the coming days, set aside time to undertake the stations of the cross. Give yourself time to consider how meditating on Christ's way of the cross sheds light on the specific struggles you are facing.

Exercise 27

Resolve

✝

The Lord GOD has opened my ear,
and I was not rebellious,
I did not turn backward.
I gave my back to those who struck me,
and my cheeks to those who pulled out the beard;
I did not hide my face
from insult and spitting.

The LORD God helps me;
therefore I have not been disgraced;
therefore I have set my face like flint,
and I know that I shall not be put to shame;
he who vindicates me is near.
Who will contend with me?
Let us stand up together.
Who are my adversaries?
Let them confront me.

—Isaiah 50:5–8

Viktor Frankl, the famous psychiatrist and concentration-camp survivor, observed in his important book *Man's Search for Meaning* that only those who had a reason to persevere in the horrific experience of the camps survived; those who lost hope quickly died. Quoting Nietzsche, he believed that "those who have a 'why' to live, can bear with almost any 'how.'" For Frankl, sacrifice is tolerable when it is meaningful.

The Evangelists portray Jesus as facing his suffering with resolve, not ignoring its reality, but choosing to enter it with his "face like flint." All four use the language of Psalm 22, described as "a poem of the person abandoned by God" or "a prayer of an innocent person." They also borrow the language and themes of the suffering servant of God, found in Isaiah, including the text above. They describe Jesus as fulfilling what Isaiah had described as a person who, in the midst of the great exile of Israel in Babylon, was called "to raise up the tribes of Jacob and to restore the survivors of Israel" (Isaiah 49:6) in order that God's salvation might reach to the ends of the earth. Jesus is faithful to his death.

Recalling the way Jesus approached his death, Paul would later write of how he himself thought nothing of the sufferings he faced.

> For I am convinced that neither death, nor life, nor angels, nor rulers, nor things present, nor things to come, nor powers, nor height, nor depth, nor anything else in all creation, will be able to separate us from the love of God in Christ Jesus our Lord.
> —Romans 8:38–39

Following Jesus, and following Paul's understanding of what Jesus' sacrifice meant, our prayer is that we might live in fidelity to our God who loves us, with perfect readiness to go where he calls us, unafraid of the consequences of that call.

Prayer

Lord, you know my fears and you yourself knew what it was to be afraid in the face of suffering. Send me the consolation of your Holy Spirit, so that I, too, can face my fears with resolve, knowing that I seek only to do what you ask. Grant me your grace even in those times when I cannot feel you near, and when I walk blindly in the hope that what I do is right.

Action

Identify a goal in your life that has been on the "to do" list but which, perhaps out of fear or some other kind of resistance, you've been avoiding. Resolve to face it with courage. Do it today.

Exercise 28

Crowning with Thorns

†

The soldiers of the governor took Jesus into the governor's headquarters, and they gathered the whole cohort around him. They stripped him and put a scarlet robe on him, and after twisting some thorns into a crown, they put it on his head. They put a reed in his right hand and knelt before him and mocked him, saying, "Hail, King of the Jews!" They spat on him, and took the reed and struck him on the head. After mocking him, they stripped him of the robe and put his own clothes on him. Then they led him away to crucify him.

—Matthew 27:27–30

Atop many crucifixes is the acronym INRI, which stands for *Iesus Nazarenus Rex Iudaeorum*, or "Jesus of Nazareth King of the Jews." The soldiers put this sign above Jesus' head on the cross (see Matthew 27:37) in a mocking description of his crime. The crowning with thorns is yet one more painful reminder that the Romans considered Jesus a funny little backwater preacher. They ridiculed Jesus and the entire community—peasant Jews—that he came from.

It is no surprise that, centuries later, Christian iconography exalted the image of *Christus victor*, Christ triumphant. Perhaps the most striking portrayal of this image is that by Tommaso Laureti, a painting completed in 1585 and called *Il Trionfo della Cristianità* (*The Triumph of Christianity*), which portrays Christ's cross in a room where the statue of a Roman god lies broken on the ground. The conversion of the Roman Emperor Constantine signaled a sea change in the public perception of the church, from persecuted sect to official religion of the Empire. "Take that, Roman imperialists!" one can almost hear the Christians say as they come out of hiding.

It is a temptation to substitute the triumph of the church for the triumph of Christ. The crowning with thorns is a difficult reminder that what Christ himself experienced was a triumph over his own fear of death at Gethsemane and a complete willingness to be killed as a result of preaching the gospel. Jesus showed no interest in politically motivated "community organizing," no taste for overthrowing the resident oppressors, no tolerance for those even in his inner circle who wanted to establish a new political order in Jerusalem or beyond. His triumph was then and is now a paradoxical one, signaled not by anything resembling victory in the usual senses. His crown was not the laurel leaf but the thorn.

What are the ways in which my willingness to follow Christ leads me to crowns of thorns, instead of to political victories? Will I witness to my faith even when I know it will be unpopular?

Prayer

Jesus, you know what it is like to suffer for telling the truth about the world the Father made. I want to follow you, but sometimes I'm afraid to be too loud about it. I want to be a good person and get along with people, but I also want to have integrity and not just go along with what I know is wrong. Help me discern how to serve you and your kingdom, how to live the truth and be willing to name the truth, but always to recognize that I must do it with the same courageous love that you showed.

Action

Bookmark and follow different Catholic news organizations. Learn how their coverage of controversial issues differs from that of mainstream media outlets.

Exercise 29

Way of the Cross

✝

A great number of the people followed him, and among them were women who were beating their breasts and wailing for him. But Jesus turned to them and said, "Daughters of Jerusalem, do not weep for me, but weep for yourselves and for your children. For the days are surely coming when they will say, 'Blessed are the barren, and the wombs that never bore, and the breasts that never nursed.' Then they will begin to say to the mountains, 'Fall on us'; and to the hills, 'Cover us.' For if they do this when the wood is green, what will happen when it is dry?"

—Luke 23:27–31

The women in this moving scene are able to see what is happening with a clarity that eludes both Jesus' disciples and the soldiers. The disciples have vanished; they are likely afraid that too close an association with a condemned man will get them into the same trouble. Peter's denial of Jesus (see Luke 22:54–62) shows evidence of this fear. The soldiers are just doing their jobs, hardened and jaded by their grisly work.

The women see, as it were, the emperor's new clothes. They see an innocent man made to suffer and die, and they are horrified. They see that he has been abandoned by his friends because they are afraid. And they wail because they know that there is something profoundly wrong in the order of things. Where is God in all this?

Luke's words here are one of a number of eschatological texts in the Gospels (that is, texts that deal with "end times"). He basically says that things are going to get worse, and that those who put their trust in the things of the world—symbolized by the hopefulness of childbirth—will face trouble. Like other eschatological texts, this one points to a foundation of Jesus' teaching: the world and everything in it belongs to God. It hangs by a thread from the hand of God, and it is thus the greatest arrogance on our part to imagine that it exists to serve us.

We have, then, a paradox: even on his way to suffer and die for them, Jesus reminds the women that there is to be great suffering among people. The world is a place where evil resides, but the world is also the place in which God accomplishes salvation. Out of this coexistence of evil and grace is born the faithfulness of Jesus. To say it differently: through his willingness to undergo suffering, Jesus patiently witnesses to the Father's intimacy with a world that people have turned to their own purposes.

Prayer

Do you see your willingness to live with suffering as an act of trust in the Father? Is your suffering a consequence of living with great love? As you meditate on the way of the cross, ask for the comfort of the Holy Spirit to help you know how your willingness to face suffering, along with the willingness of the entire body of Christ, is bringing about God's kingdom.

Action

Make a donation to those whom God calls you to love specifically. What circumstances in your life pull you to a particular area of need?

Exercise 30

Crucifixion

✝

Two others also, who were criminals, were led away to be put to death with him. . . . One of the criminals who were hanged there kept deriding him and saying, "Are you not the Messiah? Save yourself and us!" But the other rebuked him, saying, "Do you not fear God, since you are under the same sentence of condemnation? And we indeed have been condemned justly, for we are getting what we deserve for our deeds, but this man has done nothing wrong." Then he said, "Jesus, remember me when you come into your kingdom." He replied, "Truly I tell you, today you will be with me in Paradise." . . . Then Jesus, crying with a loud voice, said, "Father, into your hands I commend my spirit." Having said this, he breathed his last.

—Luke 23:32, 39–43, 46

The Evangelists offer three different accounts of Jesus' last words. In the accounts from Matthew and Mark, Jesus cries out the words of Psalm 22:1: "My God, my God, why have you forsaken me?" John has Jesus saying simply, "It is finished," referring to the ministry the Father had entrusted to him.

Luke's version here paints a slightly different portrait. Jesus expresses anguish similar to that described in Mark and Matthew, but also a trust in the loving hands of the Father. His suffering is real; perhaps, too, is his doubt about whether he has accomplished what the Father asked of him. "Into your hands I commend my spirit," he says. Take who I am; take what I have done; accept me into your loving arms, for I have nothing left to give.

In the months following the adoption of our son at eight years old, he quickly came to the habit of expressing the need to be held. "*Baobao*,"—"baby"—he would say in his native Mandarin, wanting to be picked up. There was often no particular need at the time, except the simple, unreflective desire to be held, loved, and cared for. Often, during his years at the orphanage, that need had been unrequited, and so this expression, which in other cases might seem regressive for an eight-year-old, was his way of building a sense of security with his new parents.

Luke's Jesus speaks a similar sentiment at his crucifixion. "*Baobao*," he says to his Father. What is more, he speaks it on behalf of the repentant criminal, promising him that in death he will know paradise.

Can I express this same desire to the Father? Can I face the reality of my own death—however near or distant—with this hope and trust? Can I face my sufferings and those of the people of God with the honesty that Jesus showed?

Prayer

Meditate on the words of Psalm 131 as you reflect on the story of Jesus' crucifixion.

> O LORD, my heart is not lifted up,
>   my eyes are not raised too high;
> I do not occupy myself with things
>   too great and too marvelous for me.
> But I have calmed and quieted my soul,
>   like a weaned child with its mother;
>   my soul is like the weaned child that is
>   with me.
> O Israel, hope in the LORD
>   from this time on and forevermore.

Action

Show a child in your life gratuitous affection. If you have no children in your life now, support an organization that ministers to orphans.

Fourth

I Will Live in Hope

Love is strong as death,
passion fierce as the grave.
—Song of Songs 8:6

Exercise 31

An Empty Tomb

†

When the sabbath was over, Mary Magdalene, and Mary the mother of James, and Salome bought spices, so that they might go and anoint him. And very early on the first day of the week, when the sun had risen, they went to the tomb. They had been saying to one another, "Who will roll away the stone for us from the entrance to the tomb?" When they looked up, they saw that the stone, which was very large, had already been rolled back. As they entered the tomb, they saw a young man, dressed in a white robe, sitting on the right side; and they were alarmed. But he said to them, "Do not be alarmed; you are looking for Jesus of Nazareth, who was crucified. He has been raised; he is not here. Look, there is the place they laid him. But go, tell his disciples and Peter that he is going ahead of you to Galilee; there you will see him, just as he told you." So they went out and fled from the tomb, for terror and amazement had seized them; and they said nothing to anyone, for they were afraid.

—Mark 16:1–8

The oldest copies of Mark's Gospel, likely the first of the four to have been written, end on this perplexing note. The two Marys and Salome are bewildered; they don't know what has happened or will happen. There is an enigmatic message from a stranger—presumably an angel—but there is nothing that they might expect from a God who dwells in the midst of changing history.

Sometimes the in-breaking of hope is similar. It may come upon us in the least expected ways, perhaps while we are after something else altogether. Perhaps it is already alive in us now in ways that will become clear to us only later. Perhaps our faithfulness to the God who surprises us trusts God to bring us to that clarity as long as our own efforts do not frustrate what he is up to. Perhaps our own experiences of death—whether real or metaphorical—are part of the ways in which God is laboring to bring about his kingdom.

Prayer

Whatever, wherever I am, I can never be thrown away. If I am in sickness, my sickness may serve Him; in perplexity, my perplexity may serve Him; if I am in sorrow, my sorrow may serve Him. My sickness, or perplexity, or sorrow may be necessary causes of some great end, which is quite beyond us. He does nothing in vain; He may prolong my life, He may shorten it; He knows what He is about. He may take away my friends, He may throw me among strangers, He may make me feel desolate, make my spirits sink, hide the future from me—still He knows what He is about. (John Henry Newman, *Meditations on Christian Doctrine*)

Action

Make a particular effort to praise God today. Let someone know how you appreciate him or her; offer a word of hope to someone experiencing desolation. Seek the Lord while he may be found (see Isaiah 55:6).

Exercise 32

Recognizing Jesus

✝

Mary stood weeping outside the tomb. As she wept, she bent over to look into the tomb; and she saw two angels in white, sitting where the body of Jesus had been lying, one at the head and the other at the feet. They said to her, "Woman, why are you weeping?" She said to them, "They have taken away my Lord, and I do not know where they have laid him." When she had said this, she turned around and saw Jesus standing there, but she did not know that it was Jesus. Jesus said to her, "Woman, why are you weeping? Whom are you looking for?" Supposing him to be the gardener, she said to him, "Sir, if you have carried him away, tell me where you have laid him, and I will take him away." Jesus said to her, "Mary!" She turned and said to him in Hebrew, "Rabbouni!" (which means Teacher).

—John 20:11–16

In this scene from John's Gospel, Mary Magdalene has just returned to Jesus' tomb after telling Peter and John that it was empty. The two men sprint to the tomb and make a fuss before deciding that Something Must Be Done. Mary can only sit, wait, and weep.

Jesus cannot reveal himself to the busy men; he can only reveal himself to the one who waits in her grief. She herself is too saddened to see what has happened. Only Jesus can open her eyes and turn her sorrows into rejoicing. Not long before his death, Jesus had promised his disciples:

> Very truly, I tell you, you will weep and mourn, but the world will rejoice; you will have pain, but your pain will turn into joy. When a woman is in labor, she has pain, because her hour has come. But when her child is born, she no longer remembers the anguish because of the joy of having brought a human being into the world. So you have pain now; but I will see you again, and your hearts will rejoice, and no one will take your joy from you. (John 16:20–22)

Now, Mary's heart is lifted. She cannot know what it will mean, but for this moment it will be enough that she is once again with her beloved teacher, and her fear is gone.

Prayer

Find an image or icon of Christ that allows you to see him with the eyes of your heart. Speak your heart to him. Listen to him.

Action

Express your love for someone who is a living icon of Christ: a parent, a spouse, a brother or sister, a friend. Do not let the day go by without telling this person how much he or she means to you.

Exercise 33

Do Not Be Afraid

†

After the sabbath, as the first day of the week was dawning, Mary Magdalene and the other Mary went to see the tomb. And suddenly there was a great earthquake; for an angel of the Lord, descending from heaven, came and rolled back the stone and sat on it. His appearance was like lightning, and his clothing white as snow. For fear of him the guards shook and became like dead men. But the angel said to the women, "Do not be afraid; I know that you are looking for Jesus who was crucified. He is not here; for he has been raised, as he said. Come, see the place where he lay. Then go quickly and tell his disciples, 'He has been raised from the dead, and indeed he is going ahead of you to Galilee; there you will see him.' This is my message for you." So they left the tomb quickly with fear and great joy, and ran to tell his disciples. Suddenly Jesus met them and said, "Greetings!" And they came to him, took hold of his feet, and worshiped him. Then Jesus said to them, "Do not be afraid; go and tell my brothers to go to Galilee; there they will see me."

—Matthew 28:1–10

Twice in this short text we see the words *Do not be afraid*—once from the angel and once from the mouth of Jesus. We also see two different reactions: the soldiers are petrified, while the women receive the words of the angel, who gives them the mission to comfort the brothers of Jesus.

Fear is the proper reaction to that which we cannot understand and which overwhelms us. Our natural inclination is to govern the world by carving it up into small parcels that our minds can grasp. Whatever cannot fit into our conceptualization of the world is frightening to us. In the ancient world, it was the realm of the gods; in the modern mind, it is the Unknown.

Jesus' greeting to the two Marys, though, evokes a different kind of fear—a fear that coexists with "great joy," as if it is bounded only by the dread that it cannot last. It is the fear of the person who has fallen deeply in love, afraid only that his or her joy cannot possibly last; or of the person who has just won the lottery and who fears that it must be some mistake. This fear-in-joy overtakes them even as they are in the midst of grief, and surprises them with its spontaneous power. The one whom they thought was dead is alive. If Christ lives, of what then should they be afraid?

> The LORD is my light and my salvation;
>   whom shall I fear?
> The LORD is the stronghold of my life;
>   of whom shall I be afraid?
> When evildoers assail me
>   to devour my flesh
> My adversaries and foes
>   they shall stumble and fall. . . .
> For he will hide me in his shelter
>   in the day of trouble;
> he will conceal me under the cover of his tent;
>   he will set me high on a rock.
> I believe that I shall see the goodness of the
>   LORD
>   in the land of the living.
> Wait for the LORD;
>   be strong, and let your heart take courage;
>   wait for the LORD!
>
> —Psalm 27:1–2, 5, 13–14

Prayer

Pray the words of Psalm 27 meditatively. What troubles are you bringing before God?

Action

Early Christians, in hope of the Resurrection, tended to the sick. Who are those whom you can serve without fear, in hope of the Resurrection? Name the way you can help bring about the kingdom, and work toward that hope.

Exercise 34

Road to Emmaus

†

On that same day two of them were going to a village called Emmaus, about seven miles from Jerusalem. . . . While they were talking and discussing, Jesus himself came near and went with them, but their eyes were kept from recognizing him. And he said to them, "What are you discussing with each other while you walk along?" . . . They replied, "The things about Jesus of Nazareth, who was a prophet mighty in deed and word before God and all the people, and how our chief priests and leaders handed him over to be condemned to death and crucified him. But we had hoped that he was the one to redeem Israel. Yes, and besides all this, it is now the third day since these things took place. Moreover, some women of our group astounded us. They were at the tomb early this morning, and when they did not find his body there, they came back and told us that they had indeed seen a vision of angels who said that he was alive." . . . Then he said to them, "Oh, how foolish you are, and how slow of heart to believe all that the prophets have declared! Was it not necessary that the Messiah should suffer these things and then enter into his glory?" Then beginning with Moses and all the prophets, he interpreted to them the things about himself in all the scriptures.

As they came near the village to which they were going, he walked ahead as if he were going on. But they urged him strongly, saying, "Stay with us, because it is almost evening and the day is now nearly over." So he went in to stay with them. When he was at the table with them, he took bread, blessed and broke it, and gave it to them. Then their eyes were opened, and they recognized him; and he vanished from their sight. They said to each other, "Were not our hearts burning within us while he was talking to us on the road, while he was opening the scriptures to us?"

—Luke 24:13, 15–17, 19–23, 25–32

The disciples' rhetorical question at the end of this story is not only a key to what they experienced when they encountered Jesus but also a commentary on the whole of the spiritual life. "Were not our hearts burning within us?" they ask, remembering that during most of their encounter with Jesus they did not know it was him until almost after the fact. Our lives are like that: we go from one experience to the other unmindful of Jesus' presence with us, until (if we pay attention) the moment of crystal clarity when all our previous experiences make sense. The key, of course, is awareness of how our own hearts are burning within us.

Prayer

Take time today and every day to pay attention to the movements within your heart. What causes you to feel something: longing, anger, sadness, indignation, happiness, consolation, lethargy? When have you felt your own heart burning within you? Bring these feelings right into your prayer.

Action

If you are in consolation, act with resolve, knowing that desolation will come again one day. If you are in desolation, act with the same kind of resolve, mindful that consolation will return and that you will again feel your heart burning within you. In either case, stay on the road and invite Jesus to sojourn with you.

Exercise 35

Visiting the Disciples

†

When it was evening on that day, the first day of the week, and the doors of the house where the disciples had met were locked for fear of the Jews, Jesus came and stood among them and said, "Peace be with you." After he said this, he showed them his hands and his side. Then the disciples rejoiced when they saw the Lord. Jesus said to them again, "Peace be with you. As the Father has sent me, so I send you." When he had said this, he breathed on them and said to them, "Receive the Holy Spirit. If you forgive the sins of any, they are forgiven them; if you retain the sins of any, they are retained."

—John 20:19–23

It is telling that Jesus' first words to the remaining eleven of his brothers give them a mission: just as the Father sent me into the world, so I am sending you into the world. And in a move reminiscent of Jesus' own baptism in the Jordan River (see John 1:29–34), when John the Baptist saw the Holy Spirit descending from heaven upon Jesus, Jesus sends them the Holy Spirit so that they might do what God alone can do: forgive sins.

Today we have all but lost what forgiveness of sins really means, and why it is only when Jesus sends the Holy Spirit upon the disciples that they can do it. We usually assume it means making up with someone, similar to the way we teach children to behave when they are learning to play with other children.

But there is something much more radical going on here. Recall that Jesus' forgiveness of sins gets him into trouble with the religious leaders of the day (see Matthew 9:1–8), who accuse him of blasphemy. Consider, too, his words to the adulterous woman: instead of accusing her, he simply says, "Don't sin again" (see John 8:11). Implicitly he is saying, "You have sinned." Today, such words would be completely unacceptable to many people. Our latter-day thought leaders are effectively saying that this kind of accusation is blasphemous: "Who are you to criticize someone else's choices?"

The difference between Jesus and those who want to stone the woman, though, is significant. Jesus gives the disciples the mission to do what the Father sent him to do: to name sins and to forgive them. It is absolutely necessary that they receive the Holy Spirit, because as ordinary men they simply could have no moral authority to forgive. There is a danger here: forgiveness requires a kind of moral high ground, and our human tendency is to want to use it to bludgeon others into seeing things our way—to condemn others. Our contemporary fascination with the "victim complex" masks a very subtle desire to have power over others. If we show they have wronged us, we can then claim a moral high ground and condemn their sins.

Jesus' command is radically different. He is calling his disciples to be agents of the kingdom, to forgive sins in God's name. They are not to occupy a moral high ground for the sake of condemnation; they are to go where Jesus went—the cross—and utter the same words that Luke's Jesus did: "Forgive them, for they do not know what they are doing" (Luke 23:34). The disciples' aim is not to score political points but to make right their relationship with God by releasing sinners from self-imposed prisons.

Prayer

Meditate on the words of the Lord's Prayer: "Forgive us our sins, for we ourselves forgive everyone indebted to us" (Luke 11:4).

Action

Practice forgiveness today.

Exercise 36

Doubting Thomas

†

Thomas (who was called the Twin), one of the twelve, was not with them when Jesus came. So the other disciples told him, "We have seen the Lord." But he said to them, "Unless I see the mark of the nails in his hands, and put my finger in the mark of the nails and my hand in his side, I will not believe."

A week later his disciples were again in the house, and Thomas was with them. Although the doors were shut, Jesus came and stood among them and said, "Peace be with you." Then he said to Thomas, "Put your finger here and see my hands. Reach out your hand and put it in my side. Do not doubt but believe." Thomas answered him, "My Lord and my God!" Jesus said to him, "Have you believed because you have seen me? Blessed are those who have not seen and yet have come to believe."

—John 20:24–29

Thomas is wary of an abstract idea about the Jesus whom he loved; he is cautious even about trusting the words of the men with whom he had traveled for many months as followers of Jesus. He wants to encounter the living Jesus.

For many of us—especially in the digital age, when so much information passes through our consciousness on a daily basis—religion can become an abstraction. We can be wary of those who profess it, even if they are close to us, perhaps our own parents, grandparents, siblings, or friends. Even though we ourselves may have had strong experiences of encountering God, we may have moments or even periods of doubt, particularly when religion confronts us with truths that we prefer not to espouse because they seem exclusionary or burdensome. We are like Thomas, not wanting to put our trust in an abstraction and yet still wanting to know God firsthand. We want the comfort that life means something, that love is real, that forgiveness is possible, that there is hope beyond suffering.

Thomas is blessed: Jesus meets him. The promise of the Resurrection for us is only slightly different, for if the risen Christ is indeed the only begotten Son of God, the Word of the Father, then he is present throughout creation the way a painter's hand is present throughout the canvas. Our encounter with Jesus need not be a mere abstraction; it can be as real as the touch of another human being to whom we reach out in love. Let us put our finger in Jesus' wounds, go where there is suffering, and encounter there him whom we love.

Prayer

Meditate on the face of a person who needs your love today. Let your heart feel deep compassion for that person. Pray without ceasing for him or her.

Action

Undertake one concrete act of love for that person today. Be generous in your love.

Exercise 37

Come Eat Breakfast

†

Simon Peter said to them, "I am going fishing." They said to him, "We will go with you." They went out and got into the boat, but that night they caught nothing.

Just after daybreak, Jesus stood on the beach; but the disciples did not know that it was Jesus. Jesus said to them, "Children, you have no fish, have you?" They answered him, "No." He said to them, "Cast the net to the right side of the boat, and you will find some." So they cast it, and now they were not able to haul it in because there were so many fish. That disciple whom Jesus loved said to Peter, "It is the Lord!" When Simon Peter heard that it was the Lord, he put on some clothes, for he was naked, and jumped into the sea. But the other disciples came in the boat, dragging the net full of fish, for they were not far from the land, only about a hundred yards off. When they had gone ashore, they saw a charcoal fire there, with fish on it, and bread. Jesus said to them, "Bring some of the fish that you have just caught." So Simon Peter went aboard and hauled the net ashore, full of large fish, a hundred fifty-three of them; and though there were so many, the net was not torn. Jesus said to them, "Come and have breakfast." Now none of the disciples dared to ask him, "Who are you?" because they knew it was the Lord. Jesus came and took the bread and gave it to them, and did the same with the fish. This was now the third time that Jesus appeared to the disciples after he was raised from the dead.

—John 21:3–14

The disciples are unable to recognize Jesus the third time they meet him after his resurrection—and after months of traveling with him. They know him only by the good that comes from listening to him.

The story of this appearance by Jesus is a parable. The disciples work hard and yield nothing—similar to our own efforts to make the world better. It is only when they receive the words of Jesus that their efforts bear fruit. And it is strange fruit: why doesn't he appear to them when they can feed the poor with their catch? Why doesn't he enable them to multiply loaves and fishes as he did on the mountainside? What he provides is a means to eat breakfast together. There will be time for the work of the kingdom; for now, it is enough simply to break bread with Jesus and eat fish with him.

Life after the Resurrection is not a relentless cycle of actions to change the world; it involves patient waiting for the Lord. Most important is not endless activity but willingness to wait for the Lord and simply be with him. We may be active, but our action will not bear fruit unless the Lord directs it. Wait for him.

Prayer

Pause from your action. Carve out extra time today to simply sit with the Lord, perhaps before the Blessed Sacrament.

Action

Wait for the LORD;
    be strong, and let your heart take
        courage;
    wait for the LORD!

—Psalm 27:14

Exercise 38

Faith and Works

✝

What good is it, my brothers and sisters, if you say you have faith but do not have works? Can faith save you? If a brother or sister is naked and lacks daily food, and one of you says to them, "Go in peace; keep warm and eat your fill," and yet you do not supply their bodily needs, what is the good of that? So faith by itself, if it has no works, is dead.

—James 2:14–17

Inflamed by apostolic zeal after his experience of the risen Christ, James exhorts his followers in Jerusalem to spread the light of faith. His words above recall Jesus' parable of the talents (see Matthew 25:14–30), in which a master demands that his servants invest and multiply the money he has given them. Both texts point to a basic proclamation about what faith in the risen Christ means: in a word, evangelization.

The gift of faith is oriented toward a deepening relationship with God through the imitation of Christ. It means drawing close to God's dream of what the world should be like, rooted in relationships of love and compassion and organized for the benefit of all. It therefore is necessarily a public faith, for like God himself—a unity of love between Father and Son in the Holy Spirit—our life ought to be defined by a constant overflow of love outward, not unlike a fountain of fresh water overflowing and giving life (see Ezekiel 47:1–12).

There is a basic logic here. When you fall in love with someone, you can't just quietly enjoy the new relationship privately. You necessarily want to enter that person's life, to go where the other goes and know the people he or she knows. You want to help that person and work with him or her. So, too, with God: falling in love with Christ means wanting to go where he is, in the faces of the poor and hungry, the tired and thirsty, the sick and imprisoned. You want to help him build a world in which God's perfect love for each person is matched and manifested in people's love for one another. To use James's language, you not only want the interior knowledge of faith; you also want to use that knowledge as a blueprint for building a better world through good works.

Prayer

Spend time in prayer today meditating on the way God views the world. Go higher than the "thirty-thousand-foot view" that people aim for; imagine the world from an infinite point of view. How does God see the world? Where does God need people to work, to apply their talents? How does God's view change my view? How do God's priorities challenge my priorities? Engage in a conversation with God. Where do I find him moving my heart to work? In which part of the Lord's vineyard shall I labor? Bring your feelings before him and ask him to purify your desires so that you will know only what works to undertake for his greater glory and majesty.

Action

Read the church's social encyclicals to learn how it has come to understand the work of building God's kingdom. Learn about labor, economics, war and peace, family, and human life in documents such as *Rerum Novarum, Quadragesimo Anno, Pacem in Terris, Populorum Progressio, Humanae Vitae*, and *Evangelium Vitae*. All are available by doing a Web search or looking on the Vatican's website (www.vatican.va).

Exercise 39

Vine and Branches

†

[Jesus said,] "I am the true vine, and my Father is the vinegrower. He removes every branch in me that bears no fruit. Every branch that bears fruit he prunes to make it bear more fruit. You have already been cleansed by the word that I have spoken to you. Abide in me as I abide in you. Just as the branch cannot bear fruit by itself unless it abides in the vine, neither can you unless you abide in me. I am the vine, you are the branches. Those who abide in me and I in them bear much fruit, because apart from me you can do nothing. Whoever does not abide in me is thrown away like a branch and withers; such branches are gathered, thrown into the fire, and burned. If you abide in me, and my words abide in you, ask for whatever you wish, and it will be done for you. My Father is glorified by this, that you bear much fruit and become my disciples."

—John 15:1–8

It may well be that one person can change the world, but only if that person draws many others to the same cause. Ultimately, only communities can change the world, and Jesus tells his disciples that the community that is the church—the community of faith in Jesus Christ, giving witness to the Father's love—will bear great fruit in the world.

Groucho Marx once opined that "marriage is a wonderful institution, but who wants to live in an institution?" He gave voice to a very modern concern not only about marriage but also about any institution—any established set of beliefs that have a hold on the way individuals curtail spontaneous desires for the sake of a larger whole. Our cultural exaltation of the individual often seems without limit, evincing a deep suspicion that goods sought by communities crush individual liberty and enterprise. To be sure, participation in a community is always fraught with such danger; to the extent that I pursue the collective good, I necessarily sacrifice some of my autonomy.

Jesus' counsel, then, is risky, but it is clear: the Father will prune dead branches in the church. Moreover, he will prune even healthy branches so that they

will bear more fruit. On a personal level, that counsel requires discernment. Which of my desires lead to
the great good that the Father dreams for the world?
Which desires, on the other hand, may lead to personal goods that do not serve the Father's dreams?

Dante's *Divine Comedy* illustrates a landscape of
the afterlife in which people live out the consequences of their desires. Those whose desires are,
in Augustine's words, "curved in on themselves" (see
Exercise 19) lose the vision of heaven, which should
be their compass point. Alternatively, those who let
go of self-centered desires in order to pursue greater
goods—those who still, in Jesus' words, "abide in the
vine"—are filled with the delights of beholding the
great good that God has wrought in their lives and
the life of the church as a whole.

Prayer

Pray for the intentions of the whole church, both in your local area and as expressed by the pope in his monthly intentions; do an online search for "Pope prayer intentions."

Action

Make a list of the things you can't live without. Bring it before God.

Exercise 40

God Is Love

✝

God is love, and those who abide in love abide in God, and God abides in them. Love has been perfected among us in this: that we may have boldness on the day of judgment, because as he is, so are we in this world. There is no fear in love, but perfect love casts out fear; for fear has to do with punishment, and whoever fears has not reached perfection in love. We love because he first loved us. Those who say, "I love God," and hate their brothers or sisters, are liars; for those who do not love a brother or sister whom they have seen, cannot love God whom they have not seen. The commandment we have from him is this: those who love God must love their brothers and sisters also.

—1 John 4:16–21

"Perfect love casts out fear," writes the author of this letter. He is right: those on a mission accept that there will be highs and lows, moments of exultation and moments of difficulty. What is important when one is on a mission is to keep going until it is completed, mindful that God's grace sustains us along the way.

Choosing to follow Jesus does not guarantee happiness in the way people often imagine it. Rather, it guarantees love—both the knowledge that God loves us deeply and unconditionally, and assurance that our living in love will lead us outward to share it with others. The words of Father Zosima in Dostoyevsky's *The Brothers Karamazov* are true:

> Strive to love your neighbour actively and indefatigably. In as far as you advance in love you will grow surer of the reality of God and of the immortality of your soul. If you attain to perfect self-forgetfulness in the love of your neighbour, then you will believe without doubt, and no doubt can possibly enter your soul. This has been tried. This is certain.

Happiness often will be a by-product of love, the way good feelings often are the by-product of exercise.

But we do not exercise only for good feelings, and we do not follow Jesus only for happiness. We set our eyes on the goal and pursue it with great resolve; for in the end, love is the only good worth seeking in this life or the next.

Prayer

Take, Lord, and receive all my liberty,
  my memory, my understanding,
  and my entire will,
  All I have and call my own.
  You have given all to me.
  To you, Lord, I return it.
  Everything is yours; do with it what you will.
  Give me only your love and your grace,
  that is enough for me.

—St. Ignatius of Loyola

Action

Make a plan to integrate prayer into your daily life. Do not let the experience of this period of reflection stay in the past; keep it active by finding time, resources, and support to help you abide in the vine that is Christ's body, the church. And from that prayer, plan how you will continue to discern the good toward which God is calling you to act.

Conclusion: Love, and Do What You Will

We return to the theme with which we began this book: St. Paul's suggestion that we can learn something about the spiritual life by imitating athletes' single-minded devotion to excellence. Our one desire must be for the kingdom of God, not as an abstract belief that God will do something to clean up the messes in the world, but rather as a daily conviction that God is calling me to respond in love to build a good world with him.

Why is such single-mindedness important? Because only such a strong desire can trump the thousand smaller desires that we experience day after day, each clamoring for our undivided attention the way a toddler constantly calls after his mother. "Do not keep worrying," Jesus says of our desires for the things we think we need to be happy. "Your Father knows that you need them. Instead, strive for his kingdom, and these things will be given to you as well" (Luke 12:29–31). Our hearts should focus always on the one needful thing: to love the Lord our God (see Deuteronomy 6:5; 11:1; 13:3; 30:6; Joshua 22:5; 23:11; Psalms 31:23; 116:1; Sirach 13:14; Matthew 22:37; Mark 12:30; Luke 10:27).

The goal of the spiritual exercises is the perfection of love. This is at once a hopeful and a terrifying proposition, for authentic love is far from the kind of sentimental manipulations dangled so promiscuously in various forms of entertainment. In a homily on the same text of 1 John we saw in Exercise 40, St. Augustine expounds on what divine love—the model for real human love—summons from us.

> Take a look at what we are insisting: that the deeds of men are only discerned by the root of love. For many things that may be done appear good, but do not come from the root of love. For flowers also have thorns: some actions truly seem rough or savage; but they are done for the sake of discipline when love demands it. There is one basic

command: Love, and do what you will. If you hold your peace, hold your peace out of love; if you cry out, cry out with love; if you correct, correct out of love; if you are frugal, be frugal out of love. Let the root of love be within you, so that nothing will grow but what is good.[5]

Augustine observes that sometimes love appears harsh, even mean: think of the parent disciplining an unruly child in the hope that the child will learn to overcome his selfish proclivities. Or consider the woman who knows her friend has a drinking problem, and is the only one who will confront her with the unwelcome truth. In all things, Augustine exhorts us, we must become adept at love, even "virtuosos" at love, practicing it with the same kind of fervor we find in the athlete or musician who demands perfection. Love is a harsh and dreadful thing, for it will take us to the ends of the earth, demand our money and our time, and call us to exchange our selfish habits for habits of generosity.

---

5. St. Augustine, Homily 7 on the First Epistle of John, 1 John 4:4–12, paragraph 8. Translated by the author.

It is little surprise that in an age of declining religious practice we should also see a decline in understanding and practicing this kind of love. For who would sign up for such self-sacrifice when offered in its place are abundant pleasures? I am reminded of Viktor Frankl's observation of prisoners in concentration camps: those who lost a "why" to live—those who lost meaning, who lost God—turned to the meaningless pleasure of smoking as a prelude to death.[6] In the absence of meaning, pleasure is the only thing worth pursuing. In contrast, recall that Jesus called himself the "true vine" (John 15:1 and Exercise 39). Our being grafted onto that vine will bring us good fruit, authentic love, at times harsh and uncompromising and at other times flexible and creative. At all times, though, that love will harmonize with what Christ is doing throughout the vineyard, throughout the life of the church. Why sign up for that kind of love? Because it is the very reason God has created us and the only source of our happiness. May we practice it in all things.

---

6. Viktor Frankl, *Man's Search for Meaning*, trans. Ilse Lasch (Boston: Beacon Press, 2006), 8.

About the Author

Tim Muldoon is the author of *The Ignatian Workout*, *Longing to Love*, and, with Sue Muldoon, *Six Sacred Rules for Families*, as well as other books and essays. He is a Catholic theologian who works in the Division of University Mission and Ministry at Boston College, where he has taught for many years.

Continue the Conversation

If you enjoyed this book, then connect with Loyola Press to continue the conversation, engage with other readers, and find out about new and upcoming books from your favorite spiritual writers.

Visit us at **LoyolaPress.com** to create an account and register for our newsletters.

Or scan the code on the left with your smartphone.

Connect with us through:

 Facebook
facebook.com
/loyolapress

 Twitter
twitter.com
/loyolapress

 YouTube
youtube.com
/loyolapress

Also by Tim Muldoon

The Ignatian Workout
*Daily Spiritual Exercises
for a Healthy Faith*

$14.95 • Paperback • 1979-5

Longing to Love
*A Memoir of Desire,
Relationships, and
Spiritual Transformation*

$13.95 • Paperback • 2805-6
